SERVICE TO THE SERVICES

A MESSAGE FROM HER MAJESTY THE QUEEN

The Chairman, The Navy, Army and Air Force Institutes

Please convey to all members of the Board of Management and staff of Naafi my warm thanks for their loyal message of greetings.

As your Patron, I send my sincere congratulations to you all on the celebration of your Golden Jubilee. During the fifty years of its history Naafi has given faithful and devoted service to the Armed Services at home and abroad, in war and in peace. It is a record of which you may well be proud.

My best wishes go with you for the future.

Buckingham Palace   ELIZABETH R.

Service to the Services
The story of Naafi

HARRY MILLER

NEWMAN NEAME LONDON

SBN 08 017412 4

CONTENTS

ILLUSTRATIONS

FOREWORD

ADMIRAL OF THE FLEET
THE EARL MOUNTBATTEN OF BURMA
KG, PC, GCB, OM, GCSI, GCIE, GCVO, DSO, FRS

How many of us Servicemen, or our families, really appreciate the tremendous service Naafi offers to us all? It has long been the object of unfair music hall jokes and I am delighted that Naafi has chosen to celebrate its Golden Jubilee by issuing this interesting and inspiring Jubilee history.

I have had close contacts with Naafi and used its facilities freely ever since its birth in 1921 but it was only when I became the Fourth Sea Lord of the Admiralty in 1950 and had the responsibility of maintaining contact on behalf of the Admiralty with those who controlled Naafi that I obtained a real insight into the working of this remarkable organisation. It was a privilege to work with outstanding people like Sir Lancelot Royle, Sir George Erskine, Sir Richard Burbidge and Major-General Feilden. They were most kind in explaining to me how Naafi was organised and operated and I have a happy memory of lunching with the Naafi board at Ruxley Towers twenty years ago.

My father went to sea in 1868 and in the memoirs he wrote for his children there is an absolutely horrifying account of the ghastly conditions under which the midshipmen lived at sea and the terrible food they had to eat, with no form of canteen at which they could buy extra comforts.

When he was a lieutenant serving on board HMS *Sultan* his captain was Prince Alfred, the first Duke of Edinburgh. In the autumn of 1877 the Mediterranean Fleet was stationed at Besika Bay in Crete during the crisis between Turkey and Russia. There were no shops or civilised facilities ashore and the Fleet depended upon an old store ship called *The Tyne* which made trips between Malta and Besika Bay. She was commanded by Staff Commander Vine, a quaint old fellow who could play *God Save The Queen* with a spoon on the top of his bald head or on a candle used as a 'Jew's harp'. At sea he made fancy shirts for himself on a sewing machine, to pass the time; their front was covered with a great many very narrow pleats in vertical lines and he always wore one of these when the Commander-in-Chief asked him to dinner. He was universally beloved, for he undertook personal commissions with shops in Malta for every officer of the Fleet and all these transactions were minutely entered in a large book; clearly a forerunner of Naafi!

In this history we are told of the old naval system of bumboatmen who supplied the needs of ships' companies as well as removing refuse. My father was fond of telling the tale that in one nineteenth century battleship the commander, who was the popular chairman of the ship's canteen committee, obtained his captain's approval to suggest to the committee that they should deal direct with the Army and Navy Stores. Only shareholders were allowed to deal with the Stores but many only held about £1 worth of share, which entitled them to a ticket to allow them to obtain this privilege. The commander had such a ticket and lent it to the canteen committee and persuaded them to deal with the Stores.

He was gratified to see that they got excellent goods at low prices and were doing better than they had ever done before. He was therefore painfully astonished when, at the end of six months, the committee said that they respectfully wished to thank him for the help he had been in allowing them to use his Army and Navy Stores ticket but that they would now like to go back and deal once again with the bumboatmen.

He only later came to hear that the committee, discovering from his card that he was a shareholder in the Army and Navy Stores, felt that he should have made enough profit out of their six months trading with the Stores to be satisfied, and they wanted to go back and run their supplies in the way they had always done, even though it was less good and more expensive!

Chapter One in this book gives us a fascinating glimpse of the conditions before the advent of Naafi. I joined the Royal Navy as a very young cadet in May 1913, towards the end of the life of the Tenant System when the Naval Canteen Service was run separately from the Army.

I remember when I was serving in the Grand Fleet as a midshipman in 1917 seeing the first boats with NACB painted on them and operated by the new Navy and Army Canteen Board. The NACB was a great advance on the old Tenant or Bumboatmen System and was the first step towards Naafi.

In the message I sent as Chief of the Defence Staff to be printed with the Naafi reports for 1959 I laid stress on the importance of the three-Service aspect of Naafi. From the time I took over Combined

Operations in 1941 I have been closely involved with three-Service administration and I must pay tribute to the fact that Naafi was twenty years ahead of any effort I was able to make in that direction.

I founded the Royal Naval Film Corporation just before the second world war and the money to pay for our films came essentially from the Naafi rebate in the various ships. Without this we would have had to charge men for coming to see films on board a ship, which would have been a very difficult thing to organise. So I have another reason to be grateful to Naafi.

It is not always realised that in war Naafi personnel, though not strictly 'combatants', share exactly the same dangers in the Fleet as the sailors in uniform. When my flotilla leader, the *Kelly*, was sunk at the Battle of Crete in May 1941 my Naafi manager, R. V. King, and his assistant, F. R. Martin, both went down with our ship.

One of my first questions when I formed the Supreme Allied Command, South-East Asia, was about Naafi. I was told that the only Service which was looked after by Naafi was the Royal Navy because the Army and Royal Air Force had their canteens and regimental institutes served by Indian contractors, not only in India (over which I had really no control) but it had also been agreed for Burma (which I was about to re-conquer). However, we were able to arrange that Naafi would definitely operate in the case of all operations outside these two countries, though we had quite a long while to wait.

My Army and Air Force commanders were most anxious that Naafi should be allowed to operate at the first possible opportunity. This came when we planned *Operation Zipper* to capture the Malay Peninsula and Singapore. Meanwhile the atom bomb was dropped, Japan surrendered and *Operation Zipper* was rushed ahead against no opposition. With *Zipper* went a full Naafi organisation, their personnel following up immediately the assault troops had got their footing ashore.

The supply by Naafi continued throughout the subsequent extremely difficult post-surrender operations in Malaya, Singapore, Java, Sumatra, Borneo, Hong Kong and indeed wherever our troops moved to recover Allied prisoners of war and internees, round up the Japanese forces and try to restore some sort of civilised life to the recently liberated starving populations.

The difficulties were terrific and I remember with great gratitude that Sir Lancelot Royle, the chairman of Naafi, himself paid visits to my theatre to ensure that Naafi was satisfactorily performing its task. The Naafi organisation was splendid and never failed to meet any demands we made, however urgent and varied, including provisions for many small operations which we had to stage at short notice in connection with our post-surrender duties.

A section of my staff dealt with Naafi's Expeditionary Force Institutes and Colonel Layard was the senior officer of this section in our group of headquarters in Kandy, Ceylon. I am glad to know that he is now the merchandise director on the Naafi board of management. I last saw him in Malta in 1954 when I was Commander-in-Chief, Mediterranean, and he was managing the Naval Canteen Service very satisfactorily.

In the 1960s, when I was Chief of the Defence Staff and the whole of our Defence Services were being reorganised, Naafi too took stock of itself, and as a result they were able to streamline even further their already efficient organisation. They were quick to realise the use of computers in running a supply organisation. As chairman of the National Electronics Council and a past president of the British Computer Society I have long preached the use of computers in helping to rationalise businesses. In fact, I made the first public speech about computers in this country as far back as 1946 in my presidential address to the Institution of Electronic and Radio Engineers, and I am proud to think that this Service organisation was one of the first to use computers – how typical of the foresight for which those in control of Naafi have become famous.

On the Naafi board of management today we have some of the best brains from the business world. They give their expert advice and services completely free and I should like to pay a tribute to them and their predecessors for having helped to build up a multifarious business capable of supplying the many needs of our modern Defence Forces in a most brilliant way.

The standard of living of Servicemen and Servicewomen today is increasing so much that the demands on Naafi will, in my opinion, continue to increase and become ever more important to morale. I feel sure that Naafi will meet this challenge as they have always done in the past, in this very exciting and interesting future.

Mountbatten of Burma

A.F.

CHAPTER ONE

Before Naafi

For centuries the welfare of Britain's fighting men was no one's official concern. The most paternal among the officers did what they could out of the goodness of their hearts and the depths of their pockets, and the government contributed spasmodically when their attention was drawn to the appalling conditions in which the men lived. It was not until 1st January 1921 that a permanent, officially recognised organisation was formed to provide the armed forces, in peace and war, at home and in battle, on land and at sea, with the extras that the nation's defenders deserved, over and above a bare ration and military weapons. The organisation was the Navy, Army and Air Force Institutes, better known by its initials as Naafi. It has waited for that peak in the life of institutions as well as men, a Golden Jubilee, to have its story told in full.

The pages that follow record Naafi's first fifty years. The story must in fact begin long before 1921. The creation of Naafi was the fulfilment of work done by men who were ahead of their time in understanding and compassion. The narrative must take account of their efforts to alleviate the grim conditions in which soldiers and sailors lived and fought and, miraculously, won their country's wars.

When Wellington described his men as the 'scum of the earth' he qualified the insult by expressing amazement that we had made them 'the fine fellows they are'. Both descriptions were apt. In the eighteenth and nineteenth centuries the rank and file were drawn from the lowest strata of society; the unemployed to whom the army was a last refuge, the drunks who were dragged out of the alehouse by the press gang, the delinquents who escaped the law by joining the army or going to sea. They gave the forces a bad name; no one enlisted unless he had something to hide or was not fit for a decent job, except of course in the officer ranks where the products of the playing fields of Eton found a respectable career and opportunities for glory.

They had money and were not dependent on what the commissary provided. The men had less choice. The quantity and quality of their food varied with the times and the leadership, and with the integrity of the authorities. William Cobbett, author of *Rural Rides*, discovered while in the army towards the end of the eighteenth century that the quartermaster was keeping back a quarter of the men's provisions, but this form of corruption was so widespread, even in high places, that exposure proved dangerous and Cobbett had to seek refuge in America.

According to Sir John Fortescue, author of *A History of the British Army* and of a little book *Canteens in the British Army*, which is the standard reference on the pre-Naafi period, a soldier in the early part of the nineteenth century had two meals a day; breakfast at 7.30 am and dinner at 12.30 pm and nothing more till breakfast the next day, nineteen hours later. The food was often bad as well as sparse, the bread alive with weevils and the meat stinking. At sea there was no escape, the ratings had to choose between poisoning and starvation. Soldiers in the field could live off the land if it were not too poor, or plunder what they could not afford to buy. The great commanders – Marlborough, Wellington – forbade looting and tried to improve conditions. So did Nelson who tried to cajole the State into giving a bounty to sailors, pointing out that 'the average life of a seaman is, from hard service, finished at forty-five; he cannot therefore enjoy the annuity for many years'. Soldiers were often as short-lived; in the Crimean War thousands died of starvation and exposure.

In addition to rations and loot there was a third source of provisions, the sutlers. These were mobile tradesmen who followed the troops in the field, selling food and drink. The name comes from the Dutch 'soeteler', derived from 'soetelen', *to befoul*. It reflects the sutler's low social status and corrupting influence. He found it more profitable to sell liquor than food, and his customers more inclined to drown their miseries than fill their bellies. The State was not averse to cashing in on the situation. In order to prevent the smuggling of drink into barracks, private suppliers were allowed to set up a canteen for the sale of spirits in the barrack yard. Later, the Board of Ordnance, which controlled the barracks, offered the concession by tender to contractors who paid a levy, known as 'privilege money', based on the number of men in the barracks.

Some attempt was made to control and regularise the sutler's contribution by appointing a regimental officer to supervise, and the honesty of the service largely depended on his forcefulness and integrity. The sutler was not always a parasite; indeed many campaigns abroad could not have been fought without the provisions he assembled or stole in the territory. Since meat was difficult to transport and preserve, he often supplied it on the hoof. Many a British army went into battle attended by a regiment of cattle and poultry.

The most famous camp follower of all time was a 'sutleress', Mrs Christian Ross. When her sweetheart was pressed into Marlborough's army she enlisted in the Scots Greys, fought and was twice wounded before her sex was discovered, caught up with Private Ross and married him, became separated from him at the Battle of Malplaquet and finally found his body among the dead. She rustled pigs and poultry, catered for both officers and men, had meals ready for the command after a long march and was a match for any trooper with language and fists. Though not exactly a prototype of the Naafi girl, her better qualities were a foretaste of what women could accomplish in a tough situation. Kit Ross is said, apocryphally, to have been buried with military honours at St Margaret's, Westminster.

As the nation's military commitments spread during the eighteenth and nineteenth centuries, the casual element in provisioning the troops resulted in very uneven treatment and great hardship. They were well served in India where native sutlers often outnumbered the army by ten to one, but there were few hardy entrepreneurs to follow them into the barren wastes of America. Boredom weighed on the men everywhere and only fighting and drink offered relief. Reading matter and entertainment were non-existent, except in rare cases like that of a Highland regiment stationed at the Cape whose colonel organised a keen theatrical troupe from among his men.

About the middle of the nineteenth century the public conscience began to stir, particularly after the publicity given to the appalling conditions in the Crimean campaigns. The first important change came with the transfer of the commissariat from Treasury control to that of the War Office, and the formation of the Military Train which was a rudimentary Army Service Corps. The commissariat set up butcheries and bakeries and provided tea, coffee and other groceries to the larger concentrations of troops at home and abroad. Other reforms followed. A few enlightened Members of Parliament urged the provision of sports facilities and gymnasia, and the government substituted a simple tenancy agreement for the privilege money which, though paid by the contractor, really came out of the soldier's pocket. New regulations in 1863 made canteens a regimental responsibility under a canteen committee. The changes looked better on paper than they proved in practice. Officers were inexperienced in buying; they tended to delegate the job and some abuses occurred.

One regimental canteen committee president, Captain Lionel Fortescue of the 17th Lancers, suspecting a leakage of cash, 'instituted the practice', writes Sir John Fortescue, 'of keeping a locked till in the canteen, sealing up change for the various silver coins, and insisting that every purchaser should place in the locked till the exact amount of his purchase. The contents of the till were counted every morning by an officer before the canteen opened, and it was found that the receipts were materially larger than they had been. Then, calculating the minimum of profit that should accrue to the canteen within a given number of weeks, Captain Fortescue ruthlessly dismissed every canteen sergeant who showed a lower figure.' Working with him was a capable and loyal canteen sergeant, John Gardner, who later, in the first world war, served with distinction on the Navy and Army Canteen Board.

The locked till expedient was copied by other regiments and brought the downfall of many delinquent canteen stewards. Within two years came a much more important move, the real forerunner of Naafi. Major Harry James Craufurd of the Grenadier Guards, canteen president of the regiment's depot at Caterham, was dissatisfied with the suppliers and decided, after consultation with his friends Captain Lionel Fortescue and Surgeon-Captain Herbert Murray Ramsay of the Scots Guards, that money could be saved by forming a co-operative society. With a few friends they collected four hundred pounds and founded the Canteen and Mess Co-operative Society, making a rule that the interest was not to exceed five per cent and that all further profits were to be handed to the regimental canteen as a rebate. The founders hoped that their customers would in time buy out the shareholders and that the co-operative would eventually become a buying and distributing agency for the whole army. Their comrades ridiculed the idea as Utopian; it was, in fact, barely a quarter of a century from fulfilment.

Naval canteens progressed more evenly than those of the Army from squalor to decency. To the Royal Navy, the equivalents of the Army's sutlers were the bumboats. These were floating scavengers, collecting garbage from ships in port and at the same time delivering vegetables and other provisions and any oddments the sailors might want on behalf of the local shopkeepers. They plied their incongruous twofold trade until well into the nineteenth century. Then the practice grew whereby each individual mess bought goods ashore and was allowed storage space on board by the commanding officer. In those days there was no general mess; the ship's company was divided into

Camp cooking in the Crimea, 1855

Barracks life – the officers' quarters, circa 1900
Halifax Barracks canteen, 1909

BARRACK LIFE—SKETCHES IN THE OFFICERS' QUARTERS

a number of smaller messes, each like a little household, catering for itself and buying goods from the canteen. It occurred to a now forgotten reformer that bulk buying would save money and that if the goods were retailed to the separate messes at a small profit the proceeds could be used for the common good. That was the origin of the Ship's Fund and the naval canteen more or less as we know it today.

In time firms sprang up which specialised in supplying goods to individual messes at retail prices and this was known as the 'Service System'. Some commanding officers asked their suppliers not only to provide the goods but to put their men on board to sell them. By the end of the nineteenth century this Tenant System had become standard practice and was officially recognised. A few years later the Admiralty drew up an approved list of canteen tenants.

A Tenant System was in operation in the Army too at the time of the Boer War, 1899-1902. Under this system regimental commanders invited tenders for the canteen contract and awarded them to the firms which offered the highest rebate and which were expected to staff and run the canteens. An alternative system was operated on a wider scale by district commanders, who appointed contractors to supply the goods but staffed the canteens with soldiers under their command. The Canteen and Mess Society received three of these district contracts and by 1900 had a turnover of more than a quarter of a million pounds. Lord Roberts, commanding the army in the Cape Town sector, noticed how much better served the Society's customers were than any others and offered it a contract to supply his whole army. This it did to everyone's satisfaction, till Lord Roberts linked with the forces based on Durban commanded by Sir Redvers Buller. Buller had his own canteen organisation, and the combined army needed only one. The commanders decided that that one should be the organisation already attached to the army in preference to the outside contractor. Under the title of South African Garrison Institutes it took over the entire function from the Canteen and Mess Society, which was left with whatever business it could pick up from the small forces remaining at home.

This was very nearly a disaster for the Society, which had expanded at great cost to serve Lord Roberts and was therefore deeply in debt. Fortescue had been killed in action, Craufurd was in poor health, Ramsay was in full time medical practice. At the last moment Mr J. F. Herring, philanthropist and financier, came to the rescue and guaranteed repayment of the Society's debts. Lord Fortescue, brother of Lionel Fortescue, who had always been interested in the venture,

B

became its first chairman. Within two years the Canteen and Mess Society had repaid its liabilities without calling upon Mr Herring's generosity.

After the South African war, a committee set up under Lord Grey to inquire into the conduct of Regimental Institutes, as the canteens were called, recommended the formation of a Soldiers' Central Co-operative Society much on the pattern of the Canteen and Mess Society, but the proposal was killed by official conservatism. The old contracting system remained and, with the exception of the Canteen and Mess Society and one or two exemplary contractors, bribery and corruption flooded back into the system and, as always, the soldiers suffered. The Society actually increased its financial benefit to the customer. Under Mr Charles Heygate, who had been its secretary from the start, it introduced a new system, whereby the goods were charged to the canteen at wholesale prices, the commanding officer approved a retail price list, and after deduction of the Society's working expenses from the retail profit, the whole of the balance was handed to the commanding officer.

Additional business came to the Society on the rebound from the canteen scandal of 1913-14, when the government investigated allegations of bribes passed to military customers by one of the War Office's approved firms. The investigating committee, under Lord Rotherham as chairman, included Sir W. H. Lever (later Lord Leverhulme) and Mr (later Sir) R. Burbidge. The name Burbidge was to figure prominently in the top management of Naafi in the second world war.

Meanwhile the first world war was about to break over Britain and to confront the Service ministries with problems on an unprecedented scale and for which therefore the nation was quite unprepared. In the twelve years since the end of the South African war even the lessons learnt in that comparatively minor operation had been forgotten. A large British army entered the field without any official provision having been made for an accompanying canteen system.

Fortunately the Canteen and Mess Society was still active and unique among the contractors as more concerned with the welfare of the service customers than with private profit. At the request of the War Office the Society formed a special department to cater for the Expeditionary Force and invited Sir Alexander Prince, managing director of the leading firm of canteen contractors, Richard Dickeson and Company Limited, to be honorary director of the department. The two organisations had been competitors; they were now united

in national service. Another stage had been reached in the slow
progress towards integration of the forces' canteen services under a
single authority.

The Expeditionary Force Canteens (EFC), as the new field service
was called, needed money, which the Canteen and Mess Society was
too poor to provide. The Army Council loaned £10,000, increased
later to £27,000, taken from the funds of the South African Garrison
Institutes. The absurd inadequacy of such a sum, even at 1914 money
values, to provide stock, transport, canteen premises and equipment
even for the first wave of the British army in France, is evidence of
the naivety of the military leadership upon the outbreak of what was
to prove the biggest and most destructive war in British history up
to that time. When realisation came, the Society was allowed to
borrow further money in the form of bank overdrafts and interest free
loans amounting to £720,000 guaranteed by the Treasury.

The cash was there, but the capacity of the Society and Dickeson's
combined could not immediately be stepped up to match the enormous expansion of the armed forces, and meanwhile many new
contractors found a loophole for reviving the exploitation which
had been all too common in earlier years. Therefore in January 1915
a board of control was formed to avert chaos. It drew up an approved list of contractors, fixed retail prices and laid down rates of
rebate. The chairman, representing the Quarter-Master-General, was
Sir George May who, as Lord May, was to play an important part
in Naafi during the second world war. The deputy chairman and
controller EFC was Sir Alexander Prince. Among the members was
Colonel Frank Benson, deputy controller EFC and later a leader of
Naafi in its early years. An inspectorate of canteens was formed, at
first separately as part of the Quarter-Master-General's department,
but it was soon incorporated in the new organisation under the
collective title of Army Canteen Committee.

In spite of control and inspection, some unsatisfactory contractors
remained. The Army Canteen Committee decided that the only way
to cure the abuses was to abolish the Tenant System and bring all
canteens under Army ownership and control. On 1st January 1917,
the Army Canteen Committee was registered at the Board of Trade
as a 'company trading not for profit'. It absorbed the Canteen and
Mess Society and Dickeson's and all the other contracting firms
supplying the Army in the UK. Within three months it took over all
the canteens in places abroad where British troops were stationed in
peacetime, but left the EFC in charge in the main theatres of war.

The Navy had always organised its canteen facilities independently of the Army. When the Tenant System began to break down and the reputable canteen contractors had transferred their military business to the newly formed organisation, the Admiralty decided to follow the example of the Army Council, break away from the outside contractor, and enter into partnership with the Army. The name of the central organisation was changed to the Navy and Army Canteen Board.

Though the Navy was numerically the smaller section, its seniority among the armed services was acknowledged (as it has continued to be in Naafi) by precedence in the title of the combined organisation. It remained in most other respects a very independent partner, having separate executive and accountancy staff, separate finances, and its own administration committee to control the day to day business of the naval canteens. When the Royal Air Force became a separate arm of the nation's defences in April 1918, its canteens too were absorbed into the Navy and Army Canteen Board. Lionel Fortescue's vision of a unified canteen system for the forces had materialised and the nucleus of Naafi was already in existence.

By that late hour no one was in doubt about the scale of the undertaking. The enlarged organisation was financed by an overdraft of two million pounds, rising to three million pounds, guaranteed by the Treasury. Buying was now possible on a large scale and the most favourable terms, and by 1918 the Board's turnover was more than forty million pounds in the UK alone. Even by second world war standards that would have been an impressive figure, but it was attained by slow and painful stages.

According to Fortescue, when the first contingent of the Canteen and Mess Society landed at Havre in February 1915, its transport consisted of a single Ford car to serve the canteen requirements of an army which, within a few months, was half a million strong. By 1918 the EFC had 450 vehicles on the Western Front. In the first six months of 1915 sales from the EFC depots and canteens in that theatre of war alone amounted to $3\frac{1}{4}$ million francs (£130,000 at the exchange rate of 25 francs to the £ sterling), rising to $223\frac{1}{2}$ million (nearly £9,000,000) during the second half of 1918. The total for the four years of war was not far off a thousand million francs (about £40,000,000). The number of base depots at the peak period was seventeen, serving nearly 600 branches in France and Flanders.

The difficulties were enormous and very different from those encountered in the same territory during the second world war. A comparatively small area had been fought over till it had been reduced to a wilderness of rubble and rat-infested swamps. Whole villages had been completely obliterated. The scene has been vividly described by Captain E. Vredenburg who had made a detailed inspection of the canteen services and reported in a book, *West and East with the EFC*, published in 1919. 'As far as the eye could see, lip to lip and overlapping, were shell holes of mud and filth, many filled with thick yellow water. Not a soul to be seen, not a living thing but two saddle-backed crows that only emphasised the solitude. And the silence – may I say that it could be heard? – it certainly could be felt in its dreadful oppressiveness. Not a building of any sort but smashed and demolished German concrete pill-boxes; not a tree, nothing but the debris of war implements and machinery. Shell cases by the thousands, dumps of live shells, rifles and bayonets, coils of barbed wire, ambulance stretchers, burnt out aeroplanes, overturned machine guns, gas masks, and near me, hanging to a post, a bell that was sounded on a gas attack being signalled. And beneath all this lay a hundred thousand dead.'

For mile after mile in that normally thickly populated corner of France and Belgium, there was hardly a building that could be roofed to make a canteen. Many of the forward EFC establishments were Nissen huts, erected in no-man's-land and accessible only by the hardiest motor vehicles along shell-torn roads suffering repeated bombardment. They were primitive by comparison with the clubs and rest houses in the rear, and most of those would have looked forlorn beside the comforts that Naafi was able to procure for the troops in the second world war.

Another peculiarity of the first world war in Europe was its static character. After a few months of movement, it settled down to three years of entrenchment, broken only by bloody and indecisive engagements and comparatively shallow adjustments of the line. An advance of half a mile on a thousand yard front made headline news. The front line soldiers lived in dugouts and trenches, often knee deep in mud and water. They needed such comforts as the canteen could afford to make their spell of duty tolerable. In retrospect, the corrugated walls, trestle tables and austere food may have become subjects of wry comment, but at the time they were a taste of civilization, brought at great cost in money and lives to the barbaric scene of modern warfare.

Usually the EFC forward base was situated at the nearest railhead, four to six miles from the front, an easy target for the enemy's gunners. It was a central store from which the regimental canteens drew their supplies. They would send a transport officer with a lorry and a cheque book to buy stock for the coffee bar and also fulfil special orders from officers and from company and battalion messes. The cash would be supplied by the commanding officer or by a whip-round among individual officers. The regimental canteen would supply the trench canteen under the control of an adjutant at battalion headquarters in the front line. Officers in the trenches sent orderlies to the little bar to get cigarettes and a bottle of something to keep out the chill. Unlike a commercial transaction, there was no cut for the middleman; prices at the trench bar were the same as at canteens in the rear.

Casualties were heavy among the canteen staff. When the fighting was severe they doubled as stretcher bearers or fought with the troops. Canteens had sometimes to be taken over by the military as field dressing stations. When the battle went against their own side and there was no time to salvage goods and equipment, the EFC often had to adopt a 'scorched earth' policy and burn down their buildings and stores to deny them to the enemy. Nearly seventy canteens were destroyed in the great German advance of 1918. In both world wars the canteen staff were among the last to leave when retreat became unavoidable.

Even in the quiet sectors it was not easy to find suitable conditions for EFC establishments. A handsome château at Regnière Écluse on the edge of the forest of Crécy, taken over as headquarters building, was found to have no water except rainwater, which may have been more wholesome than the piped supply in some parts of France but was not exactly palatable. EFC recruited local labour and made a pipeline to a fresh spring a quarter of a mile away. Everywhere miracles of construction were accomplished with completely untrained labour. Prisoners of war were useful and the supply increased enormously when the deadlock of the trenches was broken and the enemy was pursued over his own frontiers.

Behind the lines, EFC had bakeries, butcheries, laundries and mineral water factories. Mineral water was not simply an indulgence for troops with a palate for pop, though millions of pints of ginger beer and fruit drinks flowed into the canteens. It was a contribution to health, a safeguard against water-borne diseases like typhoid and dysentery. One of the sources was the Valroy mineral springs at Étaples which EFC took over for the benefit of the troops. EFC also manufactured much of its beer with malt and hops imported from England. Other items in this growing self-sufficiency were motor repair depots to service the successors to the old Ford car, an upholstery department to make huts habitable, and an equipment depot to replace pieces of crockery smashed and 'lost' by the million.

Behind the battle line were the larger canteens, clubs and rest houses. Some of these canteens were retail shops stocking more than two hundred items. The customer could choose from among fifty brands of cigarettes, get a cut off the joint and vegetables, fish and chips, a variety of sandwiches, cakes and buns, hot drinks and wine, including champagne, at prices which must have convinced the gourmets among the troops that even such a hideous war could have its compensations.

The waitresses were WAACs, members of the Women's Auxiliary Army Corps, seven hundred of whom were in the EFC service. They received some rudimentary but effective training. Among the questions in the examination papers quoted by Vredenburg were these: 'What change, in English silver, would you give to a customer who spent 4.80 francs and tendered a Canadian one dollar note?' 'What quantities of the following articles are required to make an eight gallon urn of tea, and how many cups should it realise? (a) Tea (b) Sugar (c) Milk.' 'How many carriage candles make one pound and what is the price per pound?' The carriage candles seem worlds away instead of a little over half a century from our own time.

Among the first people to staff military canteens with women had been Mr Reginald Stagg, one of the pre-war contractors who had gone over to the Navy and Army Canteen Board. He was put in charge of the home canteens during the war and filled the same office for Naafi on its formation. The Australian forces had reason to bless him. He had been the first canteen contractor to value their shilling at twelve pence instead of tenpence halfpenny as did most of the other contractors.

After the dirt and noise of the trenches, the clubs and rest houses were paradise. There a man could get a shower, haircut and shave, a game of billiards, books and newspapers and, if going on leave, a bed for a couple of nights at one of the leave billets. Some of the rest houses could put up as many as two hundred men and provide four thousand meals a day. Many of the clubs had pianos, and sing-songs were popular. The troops organised their own entertainments, helped by a professional in their midst, Mr Basil Dean, who was to become famous as director of ENSA in the second world war. Long before the 1918 armistice, every division, corps and army had its concert party. With a few sheets of canvas, lengths of timber, corrugated iron and unlimited enthusiasm, a stage could be improvised in a few hours or an auditorium fixed up for a show by the EFC film unit.

One of EFC's less obviously useful facilities in France was a printing works. It printed the EFC magazine, edited jointly by EFC men and WAACs, and undertook day to day jobbing work such as menus. One of them in Urdu for the Indian troops is reproduced in Vredenburg's book. The department performed at least one feat which deserves to go down into printing history. Tens of thousands of released prisoners suddenly descended on the canteens, in need of food, drink and smokes. Though they had no money EFC was willing to supply them, but they could not be allowed to swoop like locusts on the provisions. The printing department, instructed to produce half a million vouchers immediately, rose to the occasion magnificently. Within a few hours the men were handing vouchers over the counter and receiving goods to the value stated.

France was the great battlefield of the war, where the final decisive victory was won and the German surrender accepted. The British forces and EFC were involved also in campaigns in Italy, Greece, Turkey and Palestine, and East and West Africa. In Italy, as in France, but on a much smaller scale, Nissen huts were erected and fitted up as canteens and rest houses. Mobile canteens in lorries moved up to the front line, breweries and soft drink factories were established, and an ice factory delivered coolness by the ton for troops operating in the summer heat of the south. Ice was manufactured also in northern Greece. Packed in sawdust, it was delivered to the forward troops fighting around Salonika. Beer was brought to the troops from far afield; imports from Japan via Bombay augmented local production.

The intrepid EFC tried to establish canteens on the thin strip of the Gallipoli peninsula where British troops had, for a time, a fatal toehold, and every yard of the ground was raked by Turkish gunfire. A fully equipped canteen set up at Helles was blown to bits within a few days. Supplies, including a little Christmas cheer, were built up in the Aegean Islands to comfort the battered troops when Gallipoli was evacuated. A veteran of that gruelling assignment, Mr Edgar Pegg, still happily living in retirement after a life's work first with EFC and then with Naafi, was chief supply officer in the Gallipoli region, setting up canteens and marquees and helping to evacuate staff and supplies to Alexandria. Hundreds of turkeys, purchased alive for lack of refrigeration, died en route. Alexandria was outside the war zones but had its own private conflicts: EFC personnel often had to drive through communal riots to their warehouse.

Since the Suez Canal was the hinge upon which depended the British Empire's communications with its Far Eastern territories, Egypt had long been a major military and naval centre. EFC had a large establishment there employing more than five hundred of its own people, helped by eight hundred civilians from among the Egyptian and European residents. In addition to nearly a hundred canteens it ran hotels, mineral water factories and bakeries. The refreshment needs of the British troops in Palestine were also supplied from Egypt and included a string of soda fountain kiosks in the desert, where the men could get a pint of tea, coffee or lemonade for half a piastre (1¼d), and two packets of cigarettes or a slab of chocolate for a similar amount. The kiosks, many of them no more than a mile from the firing line, were supplied by camel as well as more sophisticated kinds of transport.

Mesopotamia presented more harassing disabilities than hostile gunfire. 'On the new world map,' wrote Captain Vredenburg, 'Mesopotamia should be painted black, for it has more flies to a square foot than any other country on earth.' Wherever EFC operated in the Mediterranean and the Middle East it had to fight malaria and dysentery as well as the human enemy, and large areas were the healthier for their efforts. In Mesopotamia they fitted up an odd looking steamboat, *Masoodi*, as a floating canteen plying up and down the Tigris and stopping at marching posts between Basra and Baghdad. In addition to the familiar items for the British troops, it catered for the Indians, supplying betel nut, mustard oil, special tobaccos, cigarettes and hair oils, toothpicks and cummerbunds. In Basra, EFC had a tailoring shop where native craftsmen made uniforms for army nurses.

Behind the EFC service in the field was a massive and heroic operation across thousands of miles of sea infested by German submarines. It was sustained by an organisation in Britain struggling continually to make good the losses against acute shortages and competitive demands. It had taken more than half of the four year war period to achieve an efficient system, but in the end the British forces had, for the first time in their history, a single, officially approved canteen service, without casual camp followers or mushroom contracting businesses to make private profit out of the national crisis. The most remarkable feature of the Navy and Army Canteen Board and its EFC limb was that they had accomplished their task without cost to the Treasury.

That fact needs some qualification. The government had provided staff, services, labour under contract, premises and shipping space and some initial finance. 'But every penny', wrote Fortescue, 'was paid off with interest. The soldier on active service was better cared for than he had ever been. The soldier at home enjoyed greater facilities for comfort at a smaller expense than ever before. Both obtained better value for their money than at any previous time. The country profited by the better service which the soldier was thus enabled to give and obtained that better service without any greater outlay. No contractor was enriched at the cost either of the taxpayer or the soldier. In brief, no one was the poorer for the labours of the EFC, and only the King's soldiers and sailors of all branches were the richer.' That habit of disinterested service and striving towards solvency were two traditions that Naafi inherited from its predecessor.

A service had been created and consolidated which it would have been folly to disband at the end of hostilities. Demobilisation sent millions of temporary sailors, soldiers and airmen home, but even a nation devoted to peace has to maintain adequate defences against emergency from outside. Those defence forces needed Naafi, and the framework was already in existence.

CHAPTER TWO

The Early Years

In spite of their magnificent performance in the 1914-18 war, the canteen organisations did not, like the fighting services, return home to the applause and gratitude of the nation. They ran into a bitter controversy. The storm blew up when the Expeditionary Force Canteens, their work in the field completed, were amalgamated with the Navy and Army Canteen Board.

The move was logical enough. Apart from some mopping up and the need for garrison duty in remote and troubled regions, the Expeditionary Forces had ceased to exist as such, and the EFC was due to be wound up. But it had made a large profit from the sale of goods to the troops, and opinion was divided as to what should be done with the money. Everyone was agreed that since the profit had come out of the fighting men's pockets it should be used for their benefit, but some insisted that it should be used to make good the losses involved in winding up the joint organisation. So began the quarrel of 'the canteen millions'.

Among the most powerful voices urging that the profits should be divided among the ex-soldiers were those of Lord Wolmer and *Truth* magazine. In response to the agitation the government appointed a select committee to inquire into the circumstances in which the NACB took over the assets and liabilities of the EFC and how the money had been used. The committee took a completely businesslike view of what was, in effect, a trading organisation and not either a charity or a government commitment. 'It would have been impossible', they reported, 'to wind up the Expeditionary Force Canteens without incurring losses. Goods which had been bought in wartime had to be sold in peacetime, officials had to be sent home and had to be maintained during the winding up of the undertaking. The change of policy of the government in demobilising the Army more quickly than, and on a different method from, that which had been originally intended was also certain to ensure losses by the Navy and Army Canteen Board owing to stock having been purchased on the under-

standing that demobilisation would go on slowly, but which purchases, owing to the quicker demobilisation, became useless for the
purpose for which they were bought.'

Sir William Plender, who had examined the accounts, stated in his
evidence: 'When one comes to look at the organisation as a whole,
whose turnover was a hundred and sixty million pounds sterling,
and considers that the net profits, including the rebate, came to
sixteen million pounds sterling or equal to ten per cent on the turnover, and that such profit was earned under war conditions when
buying was difficult, when sales were very often made under fire,
when consignments passed through many countries and many hands,
I think that the result – and I speak as a businessman of some
experience – is not unsatisfactory.' It was a well earned bouquet, and
the understatement at the end was no doubt not as grudging as it
appears. The ultimate benefit to the Service welfare funds from the
wartime earnings of the canteens was eight million pounds.

Other kinds of criticism were levelled against the Navy and Army
canteens, some of them grotesque and unsubstantial gossip which was
easily dismissed by the official inquiry, as for instance that 'nightly
orgies took place at Haider Pasha and that the high officials all had
unofficial wives'. But there were others which the investigators felt
obliged to take seriously. These concerned the disposal of stores without sufficient care to obtain the best possible prices. There was still
some room for improvement in catering for the troops in peace
and war.

The EFC and NACB had been *ad hoc* organisations assembled to
meet a national emergency. In March 1920, Winston Churchill,
Secretary of State for War, appointed an inter-departmental committee, under the chairmanship of Sir Archibald Williamson, to
advise on the kind of canteen organisation that would be needed for
the peacetime armed forces and whether the Army should have an
organisation of its own administered by the War Office. The committee were unanimous in recommending a joint organisation of all
three services and this was endorsed by a committee of the House of
Commons set up under Sir Samuel Roberts to help the still hesitant
government to make up its mind. The second committee was emphatic 'that the maintenance of a permanent organisation of the kind
is most desirable as a matter of policy, both because of the amenities
it affords to members of the Forces and, more particularly, because
it provides the nucleus of a service capable of immediate expansion
on mobilisation'. That second reason was significant. A vital
accessory of resistance against sudden armed attack by an enemy

must no longer be left to sutlers, sharks, muddled improvisation or the goodwill of impecunious officers.

The recommended name for the new organisation was The Navy, Army and Air Force Institutes. A comedian could hardly have chosen a more inappropriate designation; it suggested homes where battered warriors could end their days. 'Canteen' still had a beery connotation and, in spite of its use in the first world war, the organisation shared with the late Lord Roberts a prejudice against the word. The word Institute has persisted in the Corporation's official title to this day despite suggestions – the last was in 1965 – that it should be replaced with something less pedantic. It was, however, dropped from the names of the trading departments serving the Army and the RAF before the end of the second world war, when the Home Institutes Service and the Overseas Institutes Service were renamed Home Canteen Service and Overseas Canteen Service respectively (now known as Home Service and Overseas Service). The Navy needed no change; it had never used the word Institute.

Official likes and dislikes had no influence on the customer and the general public. The initials to which the cumbersome title was usually reduced looked like Naffy, easy to pronounce, familiar and unpretentious. You could love or hate Naafi but feel nothing for an institute. Except for official purposes the organisation is Naafi to its council and board of management, as it is to the troops and the general public.

On 9th December 1920, Naafi was incorporated under the Companies Acts 1908-17 as a company limited by guarantee and an association not for profit. By licence of the Board of Trade, the word Limited was omitted from the title. Naafi's official birthday, the day on which it started operations, was 1st January 1921. On that day many uncertainties about the canteen requirements of the three Services and the facilities available were ended. What had been nobody's or anybody's business was now vested in an official and legally constituted body. Its broad purpose to run catering and recreational establishments for the Forces and offer for sale goods other than those provided by the RASC for the Army and the RAF and the Victualling Department for the Royal Navy was made clear, but much of the detail remained vague. Like the nation it served, Naafi had no written constitution.

There is something to be said for imprecision. Too rigid a brief makes for certainty but leaves little room for manoeuvre. Contingencies arise where stringent rules can hold up urgent action. On the other hand, lack of definition can give rise to conflict, and over the

years, especially in the second world war, Naafi had many tussles
with other departments over duties, rights, needs and privileges.
That was part of the penalty of being a unique institution, having to
pick its way through many anomalies and avoid treading on the
sensitive toes of other interested parties stuck out in its path.

Though it was an 'association not for profit' Naafi was under an
obligation to trade profitably, not for the benefit of private shareholders, since there were none, but for the development of the enterprise and the good of the customer. The Service customer was to
benefit directly by cash rebates and discounts on his purchases and
indirectly out of the net surplus from the year's trading, the whole of
which, after making provision for reserves and contingencies, was
paid to the Service ministries for distribution to the Service welfare
funds. Those commitments still hold good. They have to be covered
out of a trading profit which Naafi has to make in conditions such
as no ordinary trader would tolerate or perhaps could survive.

Some of Naafi's work must be undertaken without counting the
cost and where a loss would be unavoidable. The management
cannot choose where Naafi shall operate, but must provide a service
as directed by defence requirements. Any loss will have to be made
good by a gain elsewhere. Not chance but *force majeure* rules the
swings and roundabouts of this extraordinary business.

Naafi's market is sharply defined. It can sell to the armed forces,
their families and others approved by the Service departments. It
has no control over the size and activities of its market. When the
Forces are increased by government decree, Naafi must expand in
proportion; when they are reduced, Naafi loses customers. It cannot
seek alternative outlets but has no complete monopoly within its
permitted sphere. Of course, it has exclusive trading rights in barracks, camps and Her Majesty's ships; but outside those closed
communities Naafi is in competition with other suppliers. Thus it
lacks much of the freedom of private enterprise without the shelter
enjoyed by a public undertaking. It is neither a nationalised industry
nor an activity of the Service departments. Its *raison d'être* is expressed by its motto *Servitor Servientium, servant of those who
serve*. It serves every branch of the Services in all scenes of action.
Wherever troops can march, ships sail and aircraft land, Naafi will
provide refreshment and comfort. It is truly a fourth arm of the
nation's defences.

Throughout these fifty years, apart from a launching loan, Naafi
has remained financially self-supporting. It took over from the NACB
a number of key people and certain assets and liabilities. The amount

by which the assets exceeded the liabilities, £887,000, was Naafi's original capital. In addition, the Corporation received a loan of £150,000 (eventually repaid) from the Royal Naval Benevolent Trust. Most of the assets were in bricks and mortar, equipment and stores. Among the properties acquired were some amusing items: the Furze Cottage Tea Rooms at Caterham, the Office for the Lady Inspector at Hythe, the Old Cattle Market, Dundee (nothing to do with the sale of livestock but a naval canteen).

From the start the State agreed to provide Naafi with its trading premises, which it does to this day. It was also supposed to provide furniture and furnishings, but its failure to do so caused Naafi a great deal of worry between the two world wars. After the second world war, and following strong representations by Naafi, the authorities agreed to let Naafi buy the furniture and furnishings and charge them to the State. Today, some of the larger items of equipment as well as furnishing are paid for by the State, for instance shop and bar counters and refrigeration, but not scales and cash registers, which Naafi provides.

The basic structure of the organisation was laid down in the original articles of association and changes in detail have been embodied in subsequent amendments. Policy control was vested in a council consisting originally of twelve members, four appointed by each of the three Service departments. They were later reduced to a maximum of eight members, two appointed by each of the Service boards and one or two as required appointed by the three Service boards jointly. They chose a president and vice-president from among their number. The council appointed a board of management, consisting originally of three civilians with commercial experience and three serving officers representing the three Services. Since then the number of civilian directors has been increased to nine, presided over by a chairman, who is also a member of the council. The executive is now headed by a full time managing director. The board of management controls the activities of the organisation and reports to the council. The operation of this two-tier structure will be described in more detail later, but one aspect of its formation deserves special mention. This is, the wisdom and foresight of the founders in deciding that if Naafi were to succeed in its double object as business and national service, its buying, catering and selling must be handled by businessmen. Today this would be obvious; it was not generally so in 1921.

The first chairman of the Naafi board of management was Sir Charles Coupar Barrie, KBE, MP, succeeded in 1923 by Lieutenant-Colonel Murrough J. Wilson, MP (knighted in 1927), who held that office till 1941. The board delegated wide managerial authority to its general manager, Colonel Frank Benson, assisted by two deputy general managers. One of these, Mr E. H. Cherry, was responsible for the Naval Canteen Service, the Overseas Institutes Service, and all central services. The second, Major A. R. G. Wilberforce, was in charge of the Home Service. The general manager dealt directly with the head of the supplies and buying department, at first Mr A. Shepherd, who was succeeded by Mr Harold Mills.

The business fell logically into three trading departments; the Home Institutes Service for the Army and RAF in the UK; the Overseas Institutes Service for the Army and the RAF everywhere abroad; and the Naval Canteen Service serving the Navy and the Royal Marines at home, overseas and in His Majesty's ships. After the second world war, when the British Army of the Rhine formed the front line of the nation's defences and Naafi's biggest single overseas commitment, a separate department was formed for the European Canteen Service. In general, the Army and the RAF shared the common services of the organisation. The Navy, though a partner, retained a measure of autonomy as it had done in the NACB, having separate executive, accounting and finances. In 1921 the manager of the NCS, unlike his counterpart in the Army and the RAF, was both a serving officer and a member of the board of management, and the two functions were not separated until May 1923.

At sea, Naafi had an elaborate pyramidal organisation. At the base was the ship's canteen committee elected by the lower deck to deal with complaints and suggestions and handle the ship's fund under the authority of the captain. The ship's committee elected representatives to the squadron committee which in turn elected representatives to the fleet committee, and fleet or port committees elected representatives to serve on a headquarters naval canteen committee, whose reports of proceedings were circulated throughout the Navy. In addition, the home ports and the marines were represented at Naafi headquarters. The representatives visited ship and shore establishments, investigated complaints and criticisms and kept Naafi and the Navy in close touch on all canteen matters.

This closely linked organisation reflected a closely knit community. The naval rating was a longer service man than a soldier or airman and his outlook was more parochial than theirs. He carried his canteen with him; it was part of his environment throughout long periods at sea, and he tended to take a more personal interest in it than did his counterpart on land.

So from 1st January 1921, the Services had a permanent servant

Officers' Mess of the 3rd Grenadiers, Boer War, 1899-1902

Headquarters of the Expeditionary Force Canteens at the Château Regnière Écluse during the first world war

Canadian infantry in the trenches at Ploegsteert, known to the troops as 'Plug Street', Flanders, 1916

to minister to needs whose importance had at last received official acknowledgement. 'The establishment of the Naafi', wrote Fortescue in 1928, 'presents itself as, on the whole, the greatest benefit that has ever been conferred on the Army.' As a soldier he could not speak for the sister services, but if they had had as articulate a spokesman he would probably have endorsed that tribute. 'Their great tradition, handed down from the EFC, is – to be all things to all fighting men.'

Housed at first at the NACB headquarters in Basil Street, London SW3, Naafi moved at the end of 1922 to its present headquarters, Imperial Court, a building of some distinction and historic interest in Kennington Lane, London, set among the Georgian terraces of Lambeth. Appropriately for a catering organisation, the building had once belonged to the Licensed Victuallers, for whom it had been built in 1836 at a cost of £14,000, as a school for 150 boys and girls in their care. The laying of the foundation stone by the Prime Minister, Lord Melbourne, representing King William the Fourth, was described with fervent verbosity in the *Morning Advertiser* by a young reporter called Charles Dickens, who a month later was to become nationally famous with the publication of the *Pickwick Papers*. 'The objects of the charity', wrote Dickens, 'are the children of decayed Licensed Victuallers, who are fed, clothed and educated. There is no degrading dress and no charity livery to remind the children of their destitution or the patrons of their munificence. Both boys and girls as well are as decently dressed as they would be were they receiving from their own parents the education which persons of their station of life usually receive. And their decent looks, healthy appearance and excellent demeanour must excite, in the breasts of their friends of the Institution, far more pleasurable feelings than the most ostentatious display could possibly awaken.' The chairman of the Licensed Victuallers Asylum – the word had not yet acquired its more sinister connotation – expressed the hope that 'the structure which is destined to rise above the stone which has this day been graciously laid by your Sovereign, will be as imperishable as the throne on which he sits'. In Naafi's care the building, with its warren of passages and disconcerting differences of level, shows no sign of perishing.

A few hundred yards from Imperial Court, in White Hart Street, now Kennings Way, stands Naafi's main London warehouse. It was planned for horse transport and no amount of modernisation could raise it to the sophisticated level of the computerised manufacturing, catering and retailing business that Naafi is today. The building is to

C

be sold as part of a large constructional and reorganisation scheme described in detail towards the end of this book.

Though the Great War was over and the armistice with Germany had been signed by the time Naafi was formed, the world was only comparatively at peace. There was small scale but bitter strife in many places, Greeks fighting the Turks, civil war in Ireland, a Fascist rising in Italy, a National Socialist (Nazi) party stirring in Germany, famine in Russia as the Soviets tried to make a nation out of a derelict giant, strikes and a mounting unemployment crisis in Britain. Egypt had kicked against the British protectorate and was soon to declare its independence; the British mandate in Iraq ended and a Hashemite Kingdom was established; but British garrisons remained and Naafi was in attendance. Other less momentous events coincided with the birth of Naafi: Earl Haig founded the British Legion, the Austin 7 car appeared on the roads, prohibition came to the USA, and an explorer found the footprints of the Abominable Snowman (Yeti) in the Himalayas. A note of cynicism and disillusion was visible in the Arts: Lytton Strachey's *Queen Victoria*, Bernard Shaw's *Back to Methuselah*, Karel Capek's *Insect Play*. The exhilaration and optimism that had followed the armistice were fading, and people began to wonder whether Britain was really going to be, as the optimistic slogan had said, 'a home fit for heroes'.

In those troubled years between the two world wars, Naafi went into action on successive fronts overseas, while developing its establishments at home. The first was in Ireland where British troops were intervening in a rebellion which raged in spite of (in some respects because of) the granting of Dominion Status to Southern Ireland. There was much clearing up to be done in Europe and Asia, and Naafi helped to lighten the burden for the forces of law and order. An Army of Occupation remained in Germany, and the accompanying Naafi establishments opened branches also in those curious loose ends left by the war – the Polish Corridor and the city state of Danzig, and disputed areas such as Schleswig-Holstein and Upper Silesia where a plebiscite had to be stage managed and prevented from degenerating into a riot. Germany was a vast distressed area with an inflationary problem which would be unbelievable today if the evidence were not preserved in souvenir currency notes brought back by the troops with face values of millions of marks and worth less than a farthing. Needless to say, the British troops paid for their Naafi purchases with a more stable currency.

Chaos had followed the break up of Turkey's hold on the Balkans and dominance of the Middle East, and the British Army's assignment in Iraq was to preserve internal order and exclude would-be invaders while a nation was being established. (Iraq was admitted to the League of Nations in 1932.) Palestine was another troubled area administered by Britain under League of Nations mandate and seething with conflict between Arabs and Jews. Naafi organised additional canteens to serve troops brought in from Cairo to keep the peace.

The conditions were sometimes very rough. One Naafi officer tells how he set up his store in a cave. Having no official transport, he had to collect the stock from the railhead by mule train and know how to pacify the beasts when they panicked at the sight and sound of the bigger beast on the track.

In adjacent Transjordan the climate was more hostile than the inhabitants. A Naafi base supplying RAF personnel in the capital, Amman, also supplied Ma'an, linked by a once-a-week railway service across the desert, and smaller outposts accessible by camel. In February 1935 the country, normally parched and barren, was swept with floods such as those regions had not experienced since Noah set sail on the plain of Mesopotamia. Roads became torrents, boulders and mud blocked the village streets, the railway line was washed away, sources of drinking water were contaminated, and homeless people trekked through the swamps carrying bedding on their heads in search of a resting place.

On the other side of Asia, too, Naafi was involved in disasters, some natural, such as a typhoon of exceptional ferocity in Hong Kong which drowned ten thousand people, others political and military, including sporadic outbursts of violence between Japanese and Chinese in northern China, following the end of the war between the two countries in the early thirties. In 1937 the Chinese bombed Japanese warships in the river at Shanghai, the Japanese retaliated with air raids on the city, and Naafi staff were cut off from their supplies and had to have military escort. Their Chinese employees were loyal and helpful throughout the troubles. Indeed, long before Naafi took over the British Forces' worldwide canteen services, and right up to recent times when the international settlements in Chinese cities were closed down, the China Station had been outstanding for the good relations existing between the local labour and their British employers.

Elsewhere in China life was more tranquil between the two world wars. Naafi had a shop and a club in the compound of the British Embassy in Peking to serve the troops guarding the building. Once a year they went to a summer camp on the Manchurian border and lived in an ancient temple near the Great Wall. It was an idyllic life, based on a feudal system which British expatriates had enjoyed for generations, but which was to die in the approaching world war.

Gibraltar had a large establishment with canteen and recreation rooms for the garrison and the Navy ashore and afloat, and grocery shops for messes, families and dockyard personnel. Malta, headquarters of the Mediterranean fleet, was another highly organised Naafi base with facilities for the Navy and the naval hospital staff, the Army, the Marines and the RAF, and shops selling a large variety of goods, from groceries to hardware and drapery, for the Service families. In the 1930s, Naafi enlarged its fleet of supply vessels at Malta with a refrigerated lighter to carry perishables from the cold store on land to the refrigerators in ships, secure from the havoc that the sirocco used to cause in transit. Aden was another peaceful post and, according to Naafi people who had spent some years there, not the social vacuum that it is often reported to have been. The British residents had formed themselves into a congenial community, a corner of a foreign field that was, if not forever, at least for many generations, England. When Naafi took over from the NACB, it improved the furnishing and decor in the Aden canteens and added to the menu such succulent reminders of home as kippers, haddock and sausages for breakfast and roast pork for dinner.

At home and overseas, in the 1920s and 1930s, Naafi did much to soften the institutional severity of its canteens, substituting for the old contractors' pull-up-for-carmen image something nearer that of a decent restaurant. Most of the canteens had uncomfortable seats, trestle tables, shelving screwed to the walls, bare wooden boards and no decoration except advertising posters pinned up by the patrons. In that gloomy environment the customer tended to forget that the food was not too bad, and 'char and wad' remained the symbol of Naafi catering as the curled-up sandwich did in the railway refreshment rooms. A large scale refurnishing scheme was a tacit recognition of legitimate grievances.

The scheme started with a single model canteen set up in each command. After a trial period the improved pattern was extended to cover the country. Modifications were necessary in some overseas stations where materials had to be suited to the climate. The list of items, for which Naafi at that time had to pay out of its own resources, conveys the magnitude of the reforms; 11,500 tables, 31,350 chairs, 16,600 armchairs, 3,400 easy chairs, 7,700 pictures, 1,180 show stands, 30 acres of floor covering and 59½ miles of curtaining. There were civilised refinements such as clocks, mirrors, frames for menus and notice boards instead of a scribbled paper hanging awry on the wall. The management at headquarters engaged a maintenance staff to keep the new furnishings in good condition. Inevitably there were acid comments as well as praise. A commanding officer about to be moved would approve the colour scheme and his successor would hate the sight of it. Naafi learnt at a very early stage that you cannot please everyone, and that if you satisfy a majority you can hand yourself a bouquet.

One of the best served Forces was the Army of the Rhine. In Germany, Naafi requisitioned hotels to house its staff, helped to supply officers' messes, and even catered for some of the deprived population, delivering lorryloads of lager for the Germans. Naafi also ran two Rhine steamers to provide outings for the troops. Like the military hierarchy, they were three-deckers, providing one deck each for officers, NCOs and other ranks. Many Germans were on Naafi's payroll at the Cologne headquarters; they had been prisoners of war interned at Alexandra Palace and spoke an intelligible but guttural Cockney.

In 1934, Naafi was appointed the official canteen organisation to serve the Saar plebiscite force, an international body formed by the League of Nations to police the area during that period of heart-searching and conflicting emotions. The Naafi contingent was under Mr R. J. Wallace who had the temporary rank of captain. The Saar had been ceded to France under the Versailles Treaty, and its people had now to decide after fifteen years whether they would remain a French province or revert to Germany. They opted for Germany in an orderly plebiscite. The proceedings took some months. Naafi provided the advance forces with cartons of tea and breakfast rations for the journey and then organised full restaurant and bar facilities in all the main towns from their headquarter offices, central stores and bakeries in Saarbrücken, and also supplied six officers' messes with messing goods, cigarettes and tobacco.

The French had waived all customs duty and railway charges on Naafi supplies, and it was therefore possible to make price concessions to the troops. As a police force, the troops were segregated from the local inhabitants in improvised and not very comfortable quarters, and Naafi provided games, brought over a concert party and showed the latest films in its own cinema. A consignment of turkeys, plum puddings and mince pies for Christmas was the subject of an amusing report in a British newspaper whose ominous implications were not immediately apparent. Mishearing Naafi as Nazi on the telephone, the reporter wrote that the Nazi organisation at

Aldershot had provided the plebiscite troops with their Christmas dinner. Hitler, who had been appointed German Chancellor a year before, and was already dreaming of world conquest, might have seen this as prophetic in his paranoiac imagination. Naafi's Saar mission was very successful, and the French Army showed their appreciation by inviting Mr Wallace and his contingent to break their journey for a sight-seeing tour as their guests on the way home.

A substantial Naafi sideline in the inter-war years was handled by its special catering branch. Naafi was called in to cater for regimental dinners and messes for annual events. For instance, at the Honourable Artillery Company's annual camp, Naafi conducted and provided waitress service for the officers', sergeants' and men's messes, and ran a canteen service in addition at an inclusive charge of five shillings a day, which covered three meals, service and the use of premises, everything except wines and spirits, which were available at the bars. The London Scottish, the Artists Rifles and the City of London Cadet Brigades made use of Naafi's expertise; the cadets got three cafeteria meals a day for an inclusive charge of one and sixpence, a fantastically low figure even at pre-second world war monetary values. Public events organised by the Forces also called for special catering; open days at military and naval stations, where Naafi provided tea for thousands of visitors; the Drag Hunt dinner, where the officers entertained the farmers on the night; and the Tidworth Tattoo, the Bisley shooting contests, the Royal Aero Club's events, the Schneider Trophy air race and the England to Australia air race. On this last occasion, when the Press turned up in force to see Amy Johnson and other famous fliers set off at dawn, Naafi provided a midnight breakfast at three and sixpence a head.

The largest of the special catering department's contracts lasted from 1931 to the eve of the second world war. This was the reorganisation of the staff catering in the five Royal Households at Buckingham Palace, Windsor, Sandringham, Balmoral and Holyrood House. The financial disaster of 1930 in the USA had a delayed but violent repercussion in the British economy, causing business failures and unemployment. King George V responded to the national crisis with an economy drive in the Royal palaces and decided to call in experts to cater for the Household staffs. He had had experience at close quarters of Naafi's work when convalescing from a serious illness at Compton Place in 1928, where Naafi had been entrusted with special duties, and it was to the Servant of the Services that he turned for help in his domestic problem. Naafi was to undertake the whole job of buying, preparing and serving food to all grades of the

Household staff, servants' hall, stewards' room, privy purse, house inspector and even the Royal chef's dining room.

To this job Naafi assigned Mr Ernest Warner, at that time assistant supervisor of bakeries, factories, catering and production, and subsequently head of the branch. Not knowing how the existing staff would react to the invasion of their stronghold, Mr Warner did not go in waving the Naafi banner, but as an outside caterer, and goods were not delivered to the Palace in Naafi packages but in plain wrappers. The supplies department had forgotten, however, that the vans bore Naafi's name in large and unmistakable lettering. No one at Imperial Court need have worried. The Royal servants and officials accepted Naafi and the Royal chef himself had no complaints.

The Palaces needed Naafi's modern touch. Many of the procedures had not changed since Victorian times. Naafi, as a large operator, was able to buy on better terms, rationalise the service and exercise sharp control of the costs from meal to meal. As a result, the cost of catering in the Royal Households was virtually halved. Mr Warner was complimented by the King and Queen and received the MVO for his services.

Every Royal occasion was attended by troops or by footmen, pages and other staff whose need of refreshment required Naafi's competence and care. So Naafi was in evidence at the weddings of Princess Marina to the Duke of Kent, and of Lady Alice Montagu-Douglas-Scott to the Duke of Gloucester; at the Silver Jubilee of King George V's reign in 1935 and at his funeral in 1936, and at the Coronation of King George VI. The Jubilee celebrations and festivities lasted for nearly three months. Naafi started its service with a luncheon party at Buckingham Palace for 1,300 members of the Royal Household staff and their friends who had come to see the procession, and its chef is reported to have produced some masterpieces of culinary sculpture. The troops who lined the route and the 1,700 naval men, who were housed in the Old and the New Horticultural Halls and whose special duty it was to man the streets around Trafalgar Square under Nelson's eye, were fed by Naafi; and so were 600 men of the Royal Artillery, dismissed at Charing Cross when the procession was over, and refreshed on the Thames Embankment with bag rations by the ever-thoughtful Naafi. The normal forces were greatly swollen by the influx of newcomers at Wellington and Chelsea Barracks and the Tower of London, and Naafi laid on additional supplies. Ten thousand special Jubilee teas were served by Naafi at local celebrations up and down the country.

All this was additional to the unspectacular routine catering at hundreds of canteens and shops in barracks, camps and ports in the UK and abroad. While it is true that they also serve who only stand and wait, it is movement that wins attention and makes a story. For instance, Naafi units had to accompany the troops on manoeuvres, load up rations at short notice, and issue them at a speed that would have given a less practised caterer ulcers. Naafi also contributed to Government hospitality, providing food at international conferences, Commonwealth gatherings, missions to settle special problems in turbulent territories, and visits by foreign Royalty, presidents, ministers and other politically important persons. With its cosmopolitan experience, Naafi was able to satisfy the most exotic tastes.

Sometimes a routine job would acquire unexpected drama. On 26th January 1932 a Naafi motor launch was delivering supplies to HMS *Adamant* which was trying to salvage the submarine M2, sunk in West Bay near Portland Bill. *Adamant*'s captain needed extra help and took over the motor launch and crew, putting salvage equipment and diving pumps aboard. For ten months Naafi men worked alongside the salvage teams, helping the divers, laying out wires for sweeping and slinging, towing 'camels' for raising the wreck, attending on the small boats in rough seas, and sharing with *Adamant* the heartbreak of having eventually to abandon the attempt to raise the lost ship. On their return to base they were granted special leave for their long and unusual tour of duty.

Hitler's reoccupation of the Rhineland in 1936, without opposition from France or Britain, sounded a warning which even a non-belligerent British government had to take seriously, and Churchill's demand for rearmament provoked some positive action as well as hostility. All three Services planned expansion. Under an Act of 1934 Naafi, which was not normally responsible for Territorial Army canteens, was expected to provide a service when the Territorials moved into concentration areas. Many Territorial Army units, especially anti-aircraft units, were given a subsistence allowance for messing instead of rations in kind, and Naafi offered guidance on a standard diet based on goods in its reserve warehouses. After the alert of 1938, not entirely calmed by the Munich settlement, Naafi arranged with the supplies directorate of the War Office for the establishment near RASC depots of supply points for the issue of messing goods. Sixty of these were being stocked when war broke out. In addition, warehouses were provided in each command to hold reserve stocks.

Reserve bases were organised for the Navy also. When the Munich crisis stimulated the Naval Canteen Service to rehearse the measures that it had planned to put into operation on the outbreak of war, the mobilisation of the fleet showed that the freedom of purchase allowed to ships' accountant officers in peacetime might not be feasible in war and that closer co-operation with Naafi would be advisable. By September 1939, the Naval Canteen Service at home had fifty-eight shore establishments, warehouses, depots, factories and canteens.

The canteens were generally inferior in comfort and appearance to those of the Army and the RAF. 'The typical naval canteen in a shore establishment at the outbreak of war', reported Mr Cherry, 'was a spotlessly clean but gloomy room with a characteristic odour mingled of beer, soap and stale tobacco. The furniture, while of excellent quality, was built for strength and not for comfort and appearance.' Perhaps sailors didn't care! That able Secretary to the Naval Office and delightful diarist Samuel Pepys, had written: 'Englishmen, and particularly seamen, love their bellies above everything else; and to make any abatement from them in quantity and agreeableness of their victuals is to discourage and provoke them.' It is certainly true that while complaints at meetings of the Headquarters Naval Canteen Committee concerned the quality and price of the food and drink, regimental criticisms were more on quality of service, comfort and appearance. The Navy did, eventually, catch up with the junior Services in appreciating less Spartan amenities.

Naafi enlarged its fleet of motor launches as war approached. In 1936 the *Imperial Club Magazine*, a journal issued from the Kennington headquarters and discontinued soon after the start of the war, reported the launching at West Looe, Cornwall, of the fiftieth NCS vessel. (The figure took into account those which had been inherited from the old contractors by the NACB.) The reporter asked, 'What type of boat will be in vogue in 1966? Will it be some sort of flying boat which can drop into White Hart Street and load up a Seastock for delivery same day to HMS *Blank* on the West Indies station?' In that particular at least, fact has not yet overtaken science fiction.

The prospect of war brought some confusion into Naafi's relations with the Service ministries and showed up the less satisfactory aspect of its vague terms of reference. Naafi was expected to be a nucleus of expansion on mobilisation but was denied the necessary permanent manpower when the emergency arose. While Hitler was overrunning Austria and planning the invasion of Poland that precipitated the war, Naafi had to plead with the authorities to be allowed to retain enough men to provide an adequate service. It pointed out that in addition to providing canteens, it was responsible for supplying about seventy per cent of the soldiers' and airmen's rations at home as well as large quantities of messing goods for the Navy, and that when war broke out a similar service would have to be organised for the Territorial Army, and for whole new conscript armies. Some years before, a percipient Under-Secretary of State for Air, Sir Philip Sassoon, had said at a Services Canteen Dinner, 'Wherever Waterloo was won, battles are now won in the cookhouse.' Napoleon had said much the same thing more than a century earlier. The lesson seemed to have been forgotten.

Not only men, but materials were lacking. On 7th September 1938, one of Naafi's deputy general managers, and the manager of the mobilisation department, were called to a conference at the War Office to discuss the question of accommodation, only to be told that no tentage or camp equipment was available for issue either at home or overseas. Further, the Army Commands had no uniform policy on the messing of the troops and could not give Naafi enough information about the disposition and strength of the units to provide a canteen or messing service. Naval mobilisation was more precise and the NCS had fewer problems, but in fairness one must recognise that the naval forces were only a fraction of the size of the Army and the requirements were proportionately more easily manageable.

In the year between Munich and the fateful 3rd September 1939 when Britain declared war on Germany, Naafi did what it could to increase its capacity. It acquired warehouses and accumulated reserve stocks. The War Department hoped to provide sixty per cent of the required accommodation in permanent buildings, and Naafi agreed to find its own canvas temporarily for the balance, until hutted canteens could be provided. As will be seen, the problems and inter-departmental conflicts dragged on until well into the war.

Naafi's grievances were genuine, but so was the dilemma higher up. Britain's characteristic unpreparedness for war had its endearing side, but it caused serious complications when the test came.

Many years before a renewed conflict with Germany was thought of, a committee had been appointed by the Army Council to examine the conditions under which the Navy, Army and Air Force Institutes would function in wartime, with special reference to the way in which the State could recover the cost of facilities granted to Naafi. This Committee on Canteen Facilities in War was reconstituted in July 1932 with broader terms of reference, to consider the financial relations between government and Naafi. The chairman of the committee was Mr B. M. Draper, CB, a director of finance at the War Office. The old controversy over the 'canteen millions' still rankled, and the Draper Report hinted that much of the profit had been made at the government's expense, and that profits in future wars must be 'really earned' instead of swollen by undercharges for services rendered by government departments. The value of the report from Naafi's point of view was that it formulated certain principles which Naafi, lacking an official code, adopted as a kind of charter in the early days of the 1939-45 war. Many of the Draper principles did not work and had to be modified or dropped, but to Naafi they offered something positive amid the general uncertainty.

The Draper principles which concerned Naafi were the following:

1. Since Naafi would be undertaking an uncommercial risk, the Treasury should guarantee it against ultimate loss.
2. Naafi's wartime policy should not aim primarily at either profit or loss.
3. The board of management should make the most effective and economical arrangements possible to provide canteen facilities and amenities at prices which the troops were accustomed to and could afford.
4. The authorised scale of wartime services and commodities should be limited to such services as were essential to the health and welfare of the troops.
5. Sales on credit should not be allowed to individuals, and sales on credit to messes should be restricted as necessary.
6. Rebate at home and in areas outside the area of operations should be continued at the ordinary rate, but no extra rebate should be paid.
7. In war areas, sales should be of three classes: (a) Sales to units in forward areas who would buy from Naafi at retail prices and run their own canteens; (b) Sales to messes at retail prices; (c) Sales to troops in non-forward areas who would use Naafi canteens.
8. No rebate would be paid by Naafi in war areas, but in the case of 7 (a) and (b) a discount of five per cent would be allowed. In the case of (c) rebate would not be paid, but would be reckoned as available to provide recreational facilities at an assumed rate of five per cent.
9. The Treasury should have the right to nominate a representative on the Naafi board.

The Draper recommendations were neither accepted nor rejected by the government, but they provided the Naafi board of management with a basis for policy. The report was an intelligent attempt to forecast wartime needs, but of course many conditions arose that no one could have foreseen. The Treasury did grant Naafi a financial guarantee. The rates of rebate recommended by Draper were reasonable and accepted by Naafi. So was the suggested limitation of credit sales. The suggestion that rebates should not be paid on canteen sales in forward areas was tried and proved unworkable; the units insisted on their 'little bit back'. Draper's idea that Naafi should aim neither at a profit nor a loss was unbusinesslike. Such an equilibrium is impossible to achieve in commerce. To Naafi the important question of policy was how to dispose of the profits. The profits could either be returned in the form of immediate benefits such as entertainment, free newspapers, free sports gear, radio, record players and so on; or handed from time to time to recognised Service charities; or accumulated till the end of the war and disposed of as directed by the Service ministries. In the light of what had happened after the first world war, no one favoured the accumulation of profits. The board decided either to forestall profits before they were earned or disburse them as soon as they became available.

Draper's idea on what was a fair price was also unrealistic. In the UK, the policy broadly laid down for Naafi by the government was to sell goods at prices which were on the whole on the same level as those charged by reputable civilian shopkeepers for goods of similar quality. When, during the war, some Members of Parliament criticised this policy, it was reaffirmed by the Treasury and the Service departments in the tenth report from the Select Committee on National Expenditure, session 1941-42. Another Draper suggestion that broke down in practice was that Naafi should place an arbitrary limit upon its services; Naafi gave as much service as circumstances allowed and the customer demanded. That was where the absence of rules helped both sides. Naafi was, throughout the war, as nearly as possible 'all things to all fighting men'.

In an appendix to the Draper Report it was suggested that Naafi should set up a separate branch to serve the forces in the field, and Naafi was at first prepared to go even further and register the branch as a separate company. This would have destroyed the unity needed for effective operation, and might have led to endless difficulties of supply and administrative squabbles. Fortunately, the Naafi board had second thoughts. When the air raid sirens howled over London for the first time on the morning of 3rd September 1939, Naafi was not exactly equipped for the desperate external struggle, but at least there was harmony within its own ranks.

CHAPTER THREE

The Second World War

On 3rd September 1939 Britain became involved in a world war against the same enemy for the second time in a generation. But only in the broadest and most superficial sense was history repeating itself. This was to prove a very different war in many ways, and at least in one small respect it was unique. For the first time in history an army was taking with it in a major war a fully organised and equipped canteen service.

The rough improvisations of earlier campaigns would no longer do. A coherent service had been created as an integral part of the armed forces. It was based on the realisation, strengthened by experience in the first world war, that morale is one of the most powerful of armaments, and must be maintained continuously if an army is to march on something stronger than its stomach. Naafi was an important contribution to morale, catering for the inner man but also for more than his basic physical needs. Its value is perhaps clearer in retrospect than it was at the time. Long after the end of the war a writer in the *Daily Mail* said, 'The Windmill (Theatre) became, along with Itma (a popular radio programme) and the Naafi, one of the three institutions that kept the nation going.'

Naafi was quick off the mark with the nucleus of an establishment in the field. Two days before the British Expeditionary Force landed in France, Lieutenant-Colonel N. V. Peters, MC, with three officers and three other ranks, left Imperial Court to set up a Naafi organisation across the Channel. They were followed within a few days by two parties totalling sixteen officers and 450 other ranks to establish base depots at Brest and at Nantes, four bulk issue stores, and canteen accommodation for 41,000 soldiers and airmen of the British Expeditionary Force.

It would be wrong to assume from that creditable start that Naafi was prepared for the trials and responsibilities ahead. No one, neither Naafi's leaders nor their masters in the Service ministries, could have foreseen the magnitude or the nature of the conflict they were to face. The comparatively uneventful early months, the 'phoney war' as it was called, delayed realisation. It was not until after the shock of Dunkirk that eyes were opened.

Nevertheless, something was done to speed up expansion and provide an organisation appropriate to the needs of war. Lacking the means in the pre-Dunkirk months to open an immediate network of canteens throughout the country, Naafi handed part of this task temporarily to private catering contractors, who ran the canteens till Naafi was able to take over. During that period Naafi continued to pay a rebate to the welfare funds of the three Services. Reorganisation had started a year before war broke out, when the Munich agreement with Hitler had bought what was obviously an illusory peace. The Home Canteen Service had been decentralised in anticipation of war. A command supervisor had been appointed to each of eight Army Commands, in each of which the Army and RAF canteens had been formed into groups further sub-divided into districts. This structure held good throughout the war. The Overseas Canteen Service was administered in London by an assistant general manager, responsible to the deputy general manager and assisted by a commercial manager. Each local headquarters organisation overseas was under a headquarters supervisor to whom the district managers were responsible. The Naval Canteen Service was slower in developing a control suited to the new conditions. The London organisation was in charge of a serving officer who had no commercial experience, and it was not until 1944 that this was made a civilian appointment.

The civilian character of Naafi as an arm of the fighting services in time of war presented several problems. At home its personnel could continue to be civilians and still serve the troops; but overseas, attached to combat forces and operating as far forward as circumstances required, the civilian status would have been anomalous. Discipline must be immediate and undivided. Also, if taken prisoner, Naafi people must have the same safeguards as combatants under the Geneva Convention. Therefore, in the field, Expeditionary Force Institutes were formed, placed under the command and wearing the uniform of the Royal Army Service Corps and designated RASC/ EFI (ATS/EFI in the case of the women). In ships of the Royal Navy they were uniformed members of the ship's complement, having been commissioned in the RNVR or enlisted in the RNR. Kipling's definition of the marines, 'a kind of a giddy harumfrodite, soldier an' sailor too,' became applicable with slight modification to the Naafi. They were service men and civilians too.

This dual status proved useful in many contingencies. EFI officers in West Africa, travelling by air from one British colony to another via neutral Liberia, would remove their military insignia, put on a civilian helmet and so escape internment. Back in the air they reversed the action and were transformed into soldiers.

In order to make their membership of the armed forces a reality, Naafi personnel had to receive some military training, but the facilities on the outbreak of war, set up hastily at Kennington, Mitcham and Croydon, were very inadequate. It was not until the end of 1940 that Naafi had its own very efficient training depot at Norwood. Many of the leaders in the field, such as Colonel Peters, had served in the first world war, but most of the personnel went out with nothing more soldierly than their uniform and their courage. The lack of training could be an embarrassment as well as a danger. Sir William Beale, who became chairman of the board after the war, recalls how he was sent out on a troopship with the rank of major to head the Naafi organisation in West Africa, and found to his dismay that as one of four majors on board he was expected to take charge of some 250 officers from captain downwards. By a coincidence, three of the senior captains proved to be old schoolfellows of his, and with their co-operation he discharged his duties as competently as his three experienced colleagues. Later, he was able to take the intensive training course at Norwood.

The RASC/EFI training and drafting depot at Norwood was established in the buildings and grounds of the Fidelis Convent. Twenty thousand Naafi officers and men passed through Norwood to the battlefields of Europe, North Africa, SEAC, and the home front in Britain. Norwood not only made soldiers out of men who had fought no one more formidable than an awkward customer in the grocer's shop, and struggled with no machine more lethal than a cash register, but prepared and dispatched the drafts, handling inoculation, complete equipment and all documentation. Naafi transport men and the entertainment branch (ENSA) all went through the mill at Norwood or one of its annexes at Hindhead and Mitcham. Long before they went overseas, they had their baptism of fire from German bombing raids on Britain.

Norwood had the honour of inspection by three successive Quarter-Master-Generals, and by Generals Sir Brian Horrocks and Sir Oliver Leese. The smartness of the Naafi forces at the passing out parades was impressive. So was the proof of their training in hundreds of emergencies overseas. It is possible here to pick out only a few incidents. At Arnhem, where a British force was besieged and under continual fire, a Naafi man had to clear a building of booby traps, hidden in innocent looking objects like clocks, before he could set up a canteen. In Malta, at the height of the bombing ordeal which won the island its George Cross, not a day passed without four or five canteens being damaged, but Naafi rescued its wounded, cleared the debris and restored the service. It even managed to co-opt a troop of cabaret girls stranded on the island, and organised the 'Whizz Bang' concert party which made up in guts what it lacked in professionalism. Captain Thomas Shannon, who had been awarded the MM in the first world war and the MC as officer commanding RASC/EFI in Crete during the second, was wounded and taken prisoner by the Nazis in 1941, and while held in various camps helped dozens of Allied soldiers to escape. Two Naafi sergeants, taken prisoner by the Nazis in Crete, escaped to the Greek mainland by fishing boat, helped to organise guerilla bands, and eventually made their way to England.

Long before Naafi had organised a training course in defence for its members, it had to think of assuring the survival of its headquarters organisation. In April 1939 the government had issued a circular advising large business organisations to move out of congested areas, especially central London, into neutral locations. Kennington was one of those vulnerable spots, and Naafi had to face strong competition for premises outside London. After much difficulty a suitable place was found at Ruxley Towers, near Claygate in Surrey. Little did they know that neither the 'wilds' of Surrey nor for that matter Liverpool, Glasgow or anywhere in these islands would be safe against air attack in a war which involved non-combatants equally with the fighting forces.

Ruxley Towers was an architectural freak, consisting of a Georgian house with a Victorian gothic tower. The tower provided a useful lookout for men of the Royal Observer Corps, scanning the sky for enemy bombers. In October 1939 most of the staff moved over from Imperial Court. The new centre, even with twenty-one huts built in the grounds, and eighteen adjacent houses taken over for hostels, was never adequate for the enormous growth of wartime Naafi. The 600-700 headquarters staff employed at Ruxley Towers at the beginning of the war had swelled to 1,100 well before the end.

As Naafi grew, recruitment became a perpetual problem. Naafi's needs conflicted with those of the armed forces and reserved occupations. Its management complained with some justification that the Ministry of Labour had completely ignored the claims of Naafi in its National Service handbooks issued just before the war. There was

The Queen's Own Cameron Highlanders in a dugout on the Somme, France, 1916

British troops receiving dinner rations from field kitchens, Ancre Area, France, October 1916

Naafi canvas camp at Colchester, 1931
Troops and their 'cuppa', 1942

a widespread assumption in official circles that Naafi should be satisfied with male staff who were too old or unfit for the fighting services. The Corporation had, in fact, lost many of its men to the Forces, and had to promote some of its older members to handle the immediate expansion; district managers suddenly becoming group supervisors and group supervisors assistant command supervisors. They rose to the occasion magnificently, but a vast intake of robust people was needed to cope with Naafi's unprecedented growth. In 1939 it had been estimated that the bulk of the British armies would remain on the Continent and that Britain, as the Forces training ground, would require fewer than 2,000 canteens to serve perhaps 900,000 men. But after Dunkirk Britain became a fortress, suffering prolonged assault of an intensity no fortress had had to endure, and needing a garrison of two million.

Many of the humbler Naafi jobs were not exactly skilled, but more training was needed than could be provided for the vast and sudden intake of raw human material. Nevertheless, educational talks were arranged at canteens throughout the country, recipes were devised, and with the help of the Empire Tea Bureau thousands of women were taught how to brew that traditional necessity, a 'cup of char' that was fit to drink; or perhaps it would be more fair to say, to do the best possible with the poor quality blends that rationing had imposed upon the home population.

The staffing problems of the Naval Canteen Services differed from those of the Army and the RAF mainly because armies are land based and fairly accessible, while ships range over thousands of miles of ocean. Naafi's naval department had to contrive its expansion from within its own small resources of long service and very experienced men, and did not employ women afloat, though they served in the shore establishments.

By badgering government departments, competing with other claimants at the employment exchanges, publicising its requirements on the advertisement hoardings and the cinema screen, Naafi built up its staff. In August 1939 it employed 5,500 people in the UK. By October 1940 the numbers had risen to 21,000, most of them women. Even before the war fifty-five per cent of the staff were women. They were eighty-five per cent by 1943.

The contribution of the Naafi girls to the comfort and morale of the Forces has never been sufficiently acknowledged outside Naafi. They came from every section of the community, waitresses and debs, service wives and teenagers straight from school, shop girls, factory girls, models and typists. They peeled potatoes and

D

scrubbed floors, cooked meals for hungry hordes at a moment's notice, served millions of cups of tea and mugs of beer, sold thousands of millions of cigarettes, kept their nerve and sense of humour under hardship and bombardment. 'They were all shapes and sizes,' wrote Monica Baldwin, author of *I Leap Over The Wall*, who had leapt from life in a nunnery to a brief spell in a Naafi kitchen, 'and they mostly came from poor homes. But they were dear people – wonderfully kind and unselfish to each other. During the shelling and bombing their attitude was one of weary contempt for the enemy. "That 'Itler," they would say. "Why can't 'e let a girl sleep?" '

They were as indomitable as hardened campaigners, often living and working in cold and cramped quarters, washing up out of doors in all weathers because there was no room in the hut, and putting up with primitive lavatories and rudimentary bathing facilities. They suffered casualties from bombing, like the rest of the civilian population. When a canteen in Oxford was bombed and many girls were seriously wounded, the rest refused to move to another location, but returned to the shattered building and put on a service amid the debris.

Inevitably, Naafi lost many of its girls by marriage. A Naafi girl never lacked an escort when off duty, but her boss made one strictly enforced rule. The soldier had to give a receipt for the girl, and deliver her back to the base by a stipulated time. The practice was neither a touching act of chivalry nor an attempt to treat women employees as chattels, but a disciplinary measure which lapsed soon after the end of the war.

At its peak period, Naafi had 60,000 women in its employment. Statistics are often dull, but the growth of Naafi during the second world war cannot be adequately conveyed without quoting figures. Between 1939 and the wartime period of greatest expansion, the number of Naafi employees throughout the world increased from 8,000 to 110,000. The number of trading establishments in all parts of the world swelled from 1,350 to nearly 10,000, including 800 canteens at sea and 900 mobile canteens. The total Naafi turnover, £8 million in 1939, was £182 million in 1945. That represents big business by any standards, but it would be even larger if translated into normal retail terms, because the sum excludes the duty on cigarettes and alcoholic drinks sold duty free to the Forces overseas.

Growth is a painful process in any kind of business, but it was particularly so for Naafi, which had to trade and provide a service under competitive conditions but without the competitive prerogative of free manoeuvre, and was denied many of the priorities enjoyed by the armed forces. Add to this the inevitable strains of administration, and the magnification of human fallibility by sudden and unprecedented demand upon individual capacities, and it is little wonder that Naafi incurred criticism in official and military circles, sometimes deserved but often due to outside ignorance of its difficulties. An inquiry into Naafi's activities by the Quarter-Master-General, General Sir Walter Venning, reported on 7th October 1940 that Naafi had been slow to change from peacetime to wartime practice, had ignored criticism, had failed to counter such criticism with propaganda when unjustified, had failed to make the institutes sufficiently attractive to the men.

Some of those strictures echoed early conflicts of policy between Naafi and the military establishment, and took too little account of the frustration of Naafi plans by official allocation of priorities. Some were justified: for instance, the first meeting of the Naafi board of management did not take place till 20th September 1939, more than a fortnight after the declaration of war, and meanwhile the general manager had had to make decisions of crucial importance. The complaints about publicity and amenities were less reasonable; in the national emergency the Naafi management had to concentrate all energies on enlarging the service, however desirable it might have been to *sell* the service. There was certainly widespread ignorance about Naafi and also damaging misconceptions: the old 'char and wads' image had by no means faded; but the days when Naafi could use public relations to good purpose were yet to come. Individuals did something to spread a new impression. Major William Beale had given a successful talk on Naafi to the troops on the ship that was taking him to West Africa. He achieved more dramatic though fortuitous publicity for the cause in a later incident. An aircraft taking him from Bathurst in Gambia to Freetown in Sierra Leone crash landed at Konakri, hit a palm tree and was too badly damaged to proceed. He radioed Freetown, a dinghy was dropped, he put out to sea and was picked up by the Royal Navy. The near loss of Naafi's West African leader brought home to thousands who had never given Naafi a thought that there was more to a canteen service than handing fags and wallop over the counter.

A month before the Venning Report was issued, the Chancellor of the Exchequer appointed a committee to consult with the Naafi management on ways of improving its service. The committee was headed by Mr (later Sir Andrew) Macharg, a chartered accountant, and Mr (later Sir) Lancelot C. Royle, managing director of the Meadow Dairy Company. The inquiry took four months, during which time the Italians invading Egypt from Libya were being driven out by Wavell; London was being bombed and Buckingham Palace was one of many buildings hit; Britain was keyed to 'fight on the beaches', as Churchill's stirring words proclaimed, if the threatened invasion were to come; and Naafi had stepped up its service of food, drink, toothpaste, shaving gear, in fact all the basic necessities and accessories of civilised living, to the staggering amount of £65 million a year. On 11th January 1941, ten days before Allied troops in North Africa captured Tobruk, the committee made an interim report, and its final report was delivered a month later.

The Macharg-Royle committee appreciated that the Naafi management had been strained almost to breaking point, that staff of military age had been snatched by the armed forces, that Naafi had not been helped to obtain staff elsewhere, and that it had been hampered in getting accommodation by 'cumbersome rules and regulations'. 'Indeed it is surprising', said the report, 'that the Corporation has been able to meet the expansion in the way that it has.'

One of the committee's fundamental criticisms was that Naafi lacked young men to lighten the burden on the senior officials and ensure succession. Those two stalwarts Sir Murrough Wilson, chairman of the board of management and an active director of the London and North Eastern Railway Company, and Colonel Benson (later Sir Frank Benson), 'father' of the canteen service and its general manager for nineteen years, were both well into their sixties and had earned some relief. On 25th February 1941 the council appointed Mr Royle as chairman of the board of management, and Mr (later Sir) George Erskine, from the merchant bankers Morgan Grenfell, as deputy chairman. Mr Erskine's appointment fulfilled the Macharg-Royle committee's recommendation that the deputy chairman should be able to bring financial experience to what was a swiftly expanding business organisation as well as a vital war service. The third civilian member, appointed by the council six months later, was Sir Richard Burbidge, managing director of Harrods. The Treasury had chosen Lord May of Weybridge to attend Naafi board meetings and hold a watching brief over the Treasury's financial commitment. The military reverses in France and Norway in 1940 had left Naafi £1,400,000 in the red, with a vast expansion programme on its hands. After long debate the government decided that Naafi should not be financed directly by the Treasury but by bank overdraft which the Treasury would guarantee. The overdraft, arranged with the Westminster Bank, had reached a peak figure of over £11 million by the middle of the war. Additional finances came from retained profits, including those from messing contracts. How Naafi's new management fulfilled their financial obligations without ultimate cost to the nation is told at the end of this chapter.

The Royle-Erskine-Burbidge triumvirate revolutionised the Naafi management structure and procedures. They appointed an executive committee of five, chosen mainly from among the existing assistant general managers and departmental heads, and promoted to deputy general managers, to handle the day to day operation. These men were the secretary and assistant general manager, Mr F. H. Crosier, responsible for Central Services and finance, who was to become the key full time figure on whom the whole organisation revolved; Mr E. H. Cherry, the only member who was already a deputy general manager, in charge of the Naval Canteen Service, the Department of National Service Entertainment and Public Relations; Mr S. Baker, Overseas Institutes Service including EFI; Mr L. C. Wynne-Tyson, Supplies and Home Institutes Service; and Mr A. L. Trundle, Personnel. The powers, duties and responsibilities of the executive committee were not strictly defined at that time; the members were regarded as 'five wise men' whose collective ability was of great value to the board. Other important figures were Mr E. F. de Lattre, chief accountant; Mr H. Mills, controller of supplies and later made a member of the executive committee; Mr R. J. Wallace, manager HIS; and Mr R. Stagg, who had handled mobilisation early in the war and was now concerned with the administration of Naafi's EFI establishments. All were answerable to the chairman or in his absence to the other two civilian members. The chairman spent three months of each year in travel, visiting Naafi organisations throughout the world, to get first hand information on conditions and needs, and maintain a visible link between the headquarters and the outposts.

Official circles were becoming aware, and Naafi's new chairman underlined the fact strongly, that Naafi ranked too low for the size of its commitment and the weight of responsibility it had to carry. For instance, it was not till the end of 1941 that any Naafi officer in the field had a higher rank than colonel, and not till mid-1943 that those three important figures Tatlow, Peters and Hamilton, of whom more will be said, were promoted to brigadier. No one at headquarters had been of sufficient seniority to meet the Quarter-Master-General. With the advent of the new board of management, Naafi ceased to be the poor relation of the services. The chairman acquired the status of Major-General, Air Vice-Marshal and Rear-Admiral in his dealings with the respective Service ministries, and had direct access to the Quarter-Master-General, the Air Member for Supply and Organisation and the Fourth Sea Lord. He preferred not to wear uniform: under a bowler hat he could remain free from protocol. Another source of strength was the fact that the chairmanship of Naafi was, and still is, an unpaid post: Mr Royle had been seconded to his wartime appointment by the Home & Colonial Group, an associate of Unilever Limited. Inevitably, there were tensions to be eased and adjustments to be made, inside and outside the Naafi ranks. It took a little time for the RASC to view Naafi as an auxiliary and not a rival. Frequent changes of personnel in the Service departments interrupted the flow of co-operation temporarily, even with goodwill on both sides. But the relationship with the Services did improve, and Naafi's contacts in the civil service were especially helpful.

The upgrading of the civilian members of the Naafi board was paralleled by that of the Service membership. The War Office promoted its member in July 1942 from Colonel to Brigadier. The Air Ministry followed suit in September 1942 by raising its representative from Group Captain to Air Commodore; and so did the Admiralty in November 1943 when it appointed a Paymaster Rear-Admiral in succession to a Paymaster Captain. Recognition of Naafi's importance as a war service was understandably belated; it was not glamorous, never directly thrust into the enemy's face, a more silent service even than the traditionally taciturn Royal Navy.

Alongside the improvement in Naafi's status and authority was a sharper awareness of its character and function. The chairman and Sir Richard Burbidge brought into the Naafi management a long and successful experience of retail trade. Naafi was a grocery and catering business. It was to become increasingly a general trading organisation. It needed men who understood the buying and selling of goods in the home and overseas markets for the personal needs of the Service man. In addition to the existing buying organisation in Australia, the board organised purchasing missions in Canada and the USA, with dollars released by the Treasury and, in the USA, also on Lease-Lend terms. Naafi paid for these substantial purchases overseas as for goods bought at home. Generous help came from the Canadian Pacific Railway, which handled the initial purchases for Naafi without charge, and then arranged that its chief purchasing officer, Mr B. W. Roberts, should act on Naafi's behalf on an honorary basis. In 1943 Mr Roberts, with Mr W. M. Neal, vice-president (and later president) of the CPR, visited Great Britain as Naafi's guests and were able to see the results of their valuable services.

As bulk purchaser and trader in non-war material, Naafi suffered from a disability which the armament buyers could not experience and did not always understand. It had to compete with other buyers in the markets for goods in short supply, and had to face restrictions on certain goods, especially rationed foodstuffs, controlled by the Ministry of Food, and a range of goods for which application had to be made to the Board of Trade. In the interests of its customers in the battlefields and on the seas Naafi would fight officialdom for priority supplies and sometimes win a concession. Then private traders would complain about this apparent favouritism, no matter how good the cause and how urgent its need. Naafi did succeed in getting priority in the fish markets, but was not allowed to exceed $7\frac{1}{2}$ per cent (later raised to 10 per cent) of the total landings on any one day. This provided only one fish meal per man per week. Naafi's egg ration was the same as that for the civilian population. The allocation was curious: two eggs a week for sailors afloat and three for RAF operational crews. Fresh vegetables were a perpetual problem, not only for sailors and for land forces on overseas stations remote from any source, but also for the large forces stationed in that far but vital corner of our own islands, the Orkneys. It would have been a sad reflection on the reality of progress if any of our men had suffered from vitamin C deficiency two centuries after a British admiral had had the brilliant idea of issuing his men with lime juice against the scurvy, and incidentally procured for his fellow countrymen the lasting nickname of 'limeys' from their American cousins.

What Naafi could not obtain at home it sought overseas or even tried to manufacture. The beer supply was a constant headache – figuratively speaking. To the troops beer is not just an indulgence but a necessity, a lubricant of morale, an extra propellant at the moment of action. The release of brewing specialists from the forces, to step up home production, and the diversion of exports to Naafi still left a gap which was partly filled by shipments from Canada, the USA, Australia, and at one time Iceland, and experimental supplies from less reliable sources. Drinkers used to say that there was beer and better beer but no such thing as bad beer; but that was before they had been drafted to the Middle East and tasted some of the local brews to which they gave unprintable names. In fairness to the local brewers it must be admitted that most of their beer was perfectly good, but of the lager type, which was unfamiliar and therefore unacceptable to British troops brought up on bitter.

Bottled beer was wasteful of shipping space, and Naafi tried wherever possible to get possession of local breweries or start brewing on its own initiative, bringing malt and barley from home if necessary.

Naafi men were wonderfully ingenious in seeking ways to ship beer economically; they tried to produce beer in concentrated, frozen, dehydrated, jellied and even powdered form, but without success. Other alcoholic drinks, especially whisky and gin, presented less of a problem because consumption was much lower, but production was curtailed because alcohol was derived from materials in short supply. As with beer, emergency supplies in the wilder theatres of war came from strange sources, and what the men could not stomach they used in their primus stoves. In some territories, where the water supply was contaminated, mineral water took precedence over alcohol, and the first thing Naafi did on landing was to set up a factory.

Tobacco and cigarettes ranked with beer as luxuries which had become necessities. The number of cigarettes dispensed by Naafi all over the world amounted to millions of millions. Here again shipping space was saved by arranging contracts near the battle area, and again not always happily. For instance, India was a useful source of supply for the troops in Africa and Asia until her government decreed that all cigarettes must contain seventy per cent of native tobacco, which British palates rejected.

Among Naafi's customers were Commonwealth troops from the white and the coloured countries, and nationals of Allied countries which had been overrun by the enemy. For them Naafi provided their traditional dishes. India had always had her own canteen services, and was one of the few major countries without Naafi; but outside their home territory, in Britain, North Africa and Europe, Indian troops used the Naafi canteens as freely as their British comrades, and had the curries and chupatties as expertly prepared as at home. Norwegians had sur sild (sour herrings) and pluk fisk (minced fish); Poles pluski (a kind of dumpling) and barsosz (beetroot soup); New Zealanders their native mutton birds brought over specially from the homeland; Canadians sweet corn, peanut butter and maple syrup; and Americans, when their own PX was not accessible, johnny cake and pumpkin pie.

Because of prohibition at home, the American troops were often short of spirits, and Naafi was regarded as a providential source of supply. Some American units were actually willing to barter jeeps for Scotch. Naafi supplied the Americans in Europe with millions of pounds worth of French and other Continental wines and liqueurs, purchased with francs or other European currencies but paid for by the Americans with dollars. Though prohibition was thus defeated behind the scenes it still reared its austere head in the official sphere. General Eisenhower, the Allied Supreme Commander, created a sensation when he ordered an issue of half bottles of champagne to celebrate victory in Europe.

One tends to dwell on food and drink when speaking of Naafi supplies, but of course there were other necessities: toilet goods and cleaning materials, stationery, newspapers and other reading matter, and articles of clothing. All were more or less restricted; for instance, Naafi could not buy shirts from the manufacturers until it had persuaded the cotton controller to release the necessary cotton. Nor was timber procurable for making shop and restaurant counters and showcases until released by the timber controller. For all its supplies to overseas stations – and to an island whatever is not home is overseas – Naafi had to find shipping space, and this was perhaps the most tightly controlled of all its requirements. Cargo ships were under continual attack, and even by mid-1943, when the number of German submarines sunk had begun to exceed their toll of Allied shipping, almost all the shipping space was occupied by war material. Naafi had to be content with 'broken stowage', filling the odd corners in a ship that were left when guns, ammunition, tanks and troops had been accommodated. This meant that Naafi cargoes had to wait till the last moment and had to be adjusted to the space available. The supplies department became adept at quick thinking and changes of plan, and at squeezing their precious goods into awkward and not easily accessible places. The legendary camel that tried to go through the eye of a needle must have been a member of Naafi transport.

It is understandable that the Service departments should regard armaments as topmost priority, though it can be argued, and Naafi did argue, that priorities are not as simple as that. The Navy was often particularly generous with shipping space; many a bottle of whisky enjoyed by the troops in Italy had travelled in the torpedo tubes of a submarine.

When the troops grumbled at the occasional monotony of Naafi meals, shortage of beer or rockiness of rock cakes, they could hardly be expected to realise what disasters had caused the breakdown, or how much effort even that deficient service had incurred. All troops must complain about something, and Naafi was a sitting target. It may be that one of Naafi's most valuable services was psychological: it provided a safety valve for accumulated tension, especially during those most trying periods when there was nothing for the troops to do except wait for action, and no enemy immediately available upon whom to vent their feelings. There was no rancour, indeed there was even a kind of affection, in the jokes at Naafi's expense; and the eagerness of the cry 'Naafi up!' when the mobile canteen appeared belied much of the criticism. In serious moments most would have endorsed the opinion expressed by Lieutenant-General Sir Brian Horrocks, who served in both world wars and was Commander-in-Chief BAOR in 1948, 'I have always been very fond of the Naafi, which somehow or other seemed to turn up when most wanted.'

Naafi came under the enemy's fire and suffered casualties very early in the war, when the land forces were still held in a 'phoney' calm. There was no lull for the Royal Navy and none therefore for the canteens on board. When a ship goes into action, so does its Naafi personnel. The sinking of HMS *Royal Oak* by a German submarine (U-boat) in Scapa Flow on 14th October 1939 involved the loss of the canteen manager and many of his staff. The first vessel to go alongside and pick men out of the sea was a Naafi canteen boat. That fact made a big impression. Five years later, the Naafi area manager at Scapa Flow had to visit the flagship of Admiral Sir Bruce Fraser, in command of the Home Fleet, on a day when such a gale was blowing in the Flow that all other shipping stayed in port. After a hazardous leap aboard the flagship he stood before the Admiral, who asked, 'How the hell did you get here?' 'In a Naafi canteen boat, sir,' was the reply. 'Yes, they never stop running,' said the Admiral. 'They were first at the *Royal Oak*.'

An even greater tribute was paid to the Naval Canteen Service after the battle of the River Plate on 13th December 1939, which resulted in the destruction of the formidable German raider *Graf Spee* by three smaller ships, *Achilles*, *Ajax* and *Exeter*. The crews of the victors were honoured by a parade in London and inspection by King George VI, and among them, representing Naafi, were two members of the canteen of HMS *Exeter*.

At the commencement of the war, the Royal Navy had some 270 canteens ashore and afloat, employing about five hundred people. They were serviced in harbour and home waters by Naafi's twenty-six motor launches (increased to forty-four by 1944), at risk from enemy submarines on their voyages round the coast and, blacked out at night, liable to be fired at in error by British naval patrols. At each of the six main naval bases in the UK, the Naval Canteen Service had warehouses, depots and canteens, and there were equivalent facilities at naval bases overseas, such as Malta, Gibraltar, Aden, Simonstown, Ceylon and Singapore. Sometimes, owing to blocked communication lines in official departments beyond Naafi's control, Naafi was ordered to start a service without having been allocated the necessary premises. However, by the middle of 1944 there were 760 NCS shore establishments at home and overseas and nearly 800 canteens in ships, which now included armed merchant cruisers.

Supplying goods to vessels whose destination, for security reasons, could not be revealed till the moment of departure, called for physical agility and mental calm, switching from tropical to cold climate packs and back again without demur. The mobility of the Navy caused temporary financial problems; for instance, how to collect the takings from canteens that might be anywhere on the high seas and absent for months. For the EFI, even in desert warfare, there was no such difficulty: the cash collector did his rounds in a vehicle like the tradesmen at the domestic back door; but the NCS credit was, geographically and tactically, unlimited.

Every ship has a space problem, and in the smaller vessels the canteen was crammed into what was little more spacious than a box. The first canteens in the smaller vessels were, in fact, converted toilets: the manager had to stand outside with his customers and reach inside for the goods. If he could squeeze inside he was almost a prisoner. 'Canteens in these ships were so small', wrote one of them, 'that when stocked up for a cruise, you opened the door, went in backwards and pulled the bottom half of the stable door behind you. There you stayed, on about one square foot of deck, until you closed.' The canteen was usually situated in the fore part of a ship, dangerous in mined waters and uncomfortable in bad weather. The staff were constantly mopping up and salvaging stores when their cubby hole was awash.

Only in the largest ships did the canteen staff have their own quarters apart from the crew. Elsewhere they shared the life of the crew, and had action stations in battle like the combatant ranks. After the 'all clear' they became caterers once more, handing out cigarettes or the traditional but now obsolete 'goffa', a soft drink consisting of a concentrated liquid diluted with aerated water. The Naafi enclave in a small ship was hardly more than a small grocery shop, but in big ships it offered such refinements as soda fountain and ice cream plant, library and bookstall.

The glamour of serving Naafi afloat outweighed the hardships, and there was never any lack of candidates for jobs. When Naafi advertised for a thousand boys for the Naval Canteen Service 35,000 applied. Many of them, straight from grocery and provision stores, were serving in a destroyer within a few days of engagement, as trainees under the canteen manager. Some of them sought adventure over and above the general hazards of their situation. On a destroyer, hunting down U-boats, a 16-year-old junior canteen assistant was the first to board the defeated enemy ship, for which he was awarded the George Medal. A canteen assistant dived repeatedly into a rough sea at night to rescue nineteen men, one for each year of his life, from a ship sunk in the Battle of Crete. Some adventures came unsought, as when Naafi survivors from the loss of HMS *Prince of Wales* towards the end of 1940, joined HMS *Stronghold*, were torpedoed by the Japanese, drifted for eighteen hours in shark infested waters and were finally taken prisoner. Inevitably, Naafi had a higher proportion of casualties at sea than anywhere else. Indeed, the casualties suffered by Naafi personnel were, in relation to their numbers, among the highest in the armed forces. More than 500 Naafi men and women lost their lives on active service.

Though Naafi people did gain military honours, their acts of courage and devotion usually took place on the fringe and not in the thick of battle, and tended to escape official notice and reward. In June 1941 Naafi instituted its own scheme of awards for gallantry, presenting an inscribed clock to the men and a gold bracelet, bearing the Naafi crest in enamel, to the women.

Naafi service accompanied the convoy escorts bringing war material across the Atlantic from America, supplying the Russians at Murmansk in the Arctic, and British land forces in the Mediterranean and other battlefields. Among the more unusual Naafi assignments was to send an official to America to provision and instal canteen managers in fifty destroyers offered to Britain on Lease-Lend terms. At home, Naafi organised and maintained a service in all the bases from which the Navy operated, from Scapa Flow to Devonport. From a supply point of view this was a more harassing job than any ordinary caterer had ever suffered or could be expected to tolerate. The Navy's movements were sudden and secret. In the Orkneys and Shetlands virtually the whole fleet would be at home one day and out on operations the next. Within twenty-four hours, therefore, the shore establishments found that 30,000 customers had melted away.

Planning for such contingencies was difficult enough, but it was a minor problem compared with that which confronted Naafi nine months after the war started, when an army of a third of a million men poured back into the south coast ports from Dunkirk. The story of that calamitous retreat and triumphant escape has been told too often to need repetition here: how the British Expeditionary Force was cut off in that north-eastern corner of France by the German advance through Belgium and the collapse of French resistance; how the survivors, massed on the beaches and wading into the water, bombed and machine gunned by German aircraft, were picked up and brought home by every kind of vessel the rescuers could muster, from warships and merchantmen to Thames pleasure steamers and privately owned rowing boats. What is not at all well known is the part played by the Home Canteen Service in providing shelter and food in an emergency without precedent in war.

Up to the evacuation, Naafi had established depots, canteens and other amenities to serve an expected battle area stretching from Flanders to Paris, and including a leave centre at the Hotel Moderne in the French capital. When the attack came through Belgium, many RASC/EFI personnel found themselves in the front line, carrying supplies to forward troops who were trying desperately to hold a position. Communications soon broke down, and Naafi units had to make their own decisions and find their own way out of the trap. They were reluctant to abandon their posts, ignoring verbal instructions to evacuate, and hanging on at Arras till the large warehouse there had been cut off by the enemy's advance. They salvaged as much material as they could and sent it in whatever lorries they could find to assembly points on the Breton coast, where ships were waiting to transport the goods to England. Some did get through. A bonded warehouse was opened in Glasgow to receive bonded stores returned from Europe, and for the first time in the history of His Majesty's Customs everything was accepted without question. But most of the material snatched from the path of the enemy was lost in a further disaster. SS *Lancastria*, carrying Naafi men and goods, was bombed and sank within twenty minutes in St Nazaire harbour. Naafi's losses at Dunkirk were heavy: 109 men killed, 57 taken prisoner and more than a million pounds worth of goods lost.

There were some remarkable acts of devotion to duty. Canteen managers staggered into the reception depots with the account books and the familiar black boxes containing the takings in francs to a total value of several hundred thousand pounds. They could have dumped the load or spent the money during the trek through the French countryside, and in the circumstances no one would have been the wiser, though the man immediately concerned would have been the sadder. In his code of conduct, the weekly cash reconciliation had to be correct, and seen to be so. These incidents occurred in other theatres of war, in Singapore, for instance, and in the Western Desert where the fluctuations of war often required the abandonment of positions as precipitately as in France. A comparable incident occurred at the time of the Japanese attack on Pearl Harbor, when Japanese aircraft bombed ships of the Royal Navy off the coast of Ceylon. A Naafi officer, whose stores and equipment had sunk with his ship, swam ashore clutching a waterproof bag containing the canteen records. Accountancy has its heroes even though armed with nothing sharper than a pen.

When the troops from Dunkirk landed in England something had to be done quickly to house and feed them. Fortunately the weather was favourable; it was the beginning of June, and the men could be accommodated temporarily under canvas. It fell to Naafi, not the War Department, to provide 800 marquees, a supply of messing goods and bag rations for men on the move. The size of the task can be gathered from the figures: there were 211,532 fit men of the British Forces, 13,053 casualties, and 112,546 French and Belgian troops. Naafi had to revise its plans, find premises for many more warehouses and canteens, enlarge enormously its purchasing and recruitment. The returned troops were not, of course, to remain long out of action, but the total British commitment had swelled from a small force in a single sector to a worldwide conflict which at its peak was to involve five million men; and the Naafi home base had to be adequate to cater not only for the home garrisons but for millions of soldiers, sailors and airmen from a dozen Allied countries in addition to our own on leave and in transit.

While coping with the aftermath of Dunkirk, Naafi had to give serious attention to the danger of invasion. This involved a redisposition of staff and establishments, in particular the removal of women canteen workers from the coast and their accommodation in tented camps prepared in advance on Salisbury Plain and other parts of the country considered remote enough in the comparatively innocent months before the Battle of Britain. Closing down a canteen or store and opening up elsewhere was not simply a matter of transferring goods and people. It was often more economical but not less complicated to dispose of goods in the one and re-stock the other; and even under the rule of war civilians were not infinitely mobile. Within seven months of Dunkirk the number of canteens in the UK had doubled from 1,800 to more than 3,600, and by June 1942 the number had trebled. At one time canteens were being set up at the rate of 100 a week.

Naafi acquired bakeries, some of them in Nissen huts, and at one time employed 1,500 people in nearly fifty bakeries throughout the country. It opened sausage factories and became largely self-sufficient in providing the troops with hot snacks: meat and potato rolls, sausages and mash, steak pie and fish and chips. The demand was heavy: troops were much less well fed than they are today. They even enjoyed Nelson cake, familiarly known as 'depth charges'. This was a Naafi expedient for saving waste at a time of food shortage. It was made out of stale pastry, layered with jam and topped with coconut – a good filler and inexpensive like most of Naafi's basic supplies. Tea at 1d a cup and coffee at 1½d were cheap even by the standards of the day; so was apple pie at 2d a portion, and a kit for making one's own cigarettes, complete with cigarette paper, at 6d.

That is the brighter side of the picture, but it must not be allowed to give an impression of consistently swift and efficient progress. 'Blood, tears, toil and sweat' were incurred in the provision of amenities as in the achievement of military victory. The Naafi Club was still to come. London had Service clubs of a kind, but for several years many provincial cities lacked suitable places where troops, passing through or on leave, could spend a few hours in comfort. No one was to blame for the delay in improving amenities. The responsibility for providing buildings was the State's and not Naafi's, but there were many calls upon the limited accommodation and the loss of premises by bombing was heavy. The canteens in barracks and camps and on airfields were certainly not good enough in the early years of the war, but they were for the most part the best possible in a nation under siege at home and suffering reverses overseas.

The siege was mounted in two elements, by U-boat attack on the supply lines and bombing from the air. Two months after the last boatload of Dunkirk survivors had reached our shores, the Battle of Britain started. It was the first great air battle in any war and resulted in a decisive defeat for the Germans. Though bombing attacks on British ports, shipping, airfields and civilian population were to continue throughout the war, the main assault had lost its impetus by the end of October, when the enemy had lost 2,375 aircraft to the British 733, and abandoned his plans to follow up with a seaborne invasion. Naafi provided a canteen service at the main RAF stations, but there was an urgent need for mobile canteens for the smaller units and the more remote locations where a static canteen could not be provided. Urged by the Air Ministry, Naafi bought a hundred secondhand chassis, had suitable bodies built on to them, and started a mobile service in October 1940. The plan eventually to have 400 or 500 of these units, carrying refreshments and the lighter luxuries to every corner of the country, was frustrated by the difficulty of getting enough vehicles, and there were never more than 380 mobile canteens operating in the UK.

Victory in the Battle of Britain saved the country from invasion, but Naafi and its customers had little respite from bombardment. Canteens on airfields, anti-aircraft gun sites and searchlight positions in the south-east corner of England continued to give a service under shellfire from the French coast as well as bombardment from the air, and the staff rejected a proposal that they should be moved to a less exposed part of the country. The same sector was the front line of defence in a second battle of Britain, when the Germans from 1944 to 1945 sought to cripple London with their flying bombs. Again Naafi stood by with a service, better equipped and organised this time, for the RAF and the people, a large proportion of them women, maintaining the balloon barrage defences.

After the fall of France and the Battle of Britain the main emphasis of the war shifted to the Mediterranean. Gibraltar, impregnable from the sea, was vulnerable on the landward side, and it was thought that the Germans might invade through Spain. Sappers and miners prepared the Rock for a siege, women and children were evacuated, and Naafi took over two hotels to provide a meal service for the remaining male civilian population. Supplies fluctuated with the success of the convoys in evading the enemy submarines; crews said there was a fifty-fifty chance of 'getting your shirt wet'. Life in that small target was noisy and nerve-racking: it was bombed repeatedly by Italian planes. The only relief was provided by concert parties from Spain and shows by Ensa, who came over, at great risk, from England, and were liable to be marooned on the Rock by enemy action.

Holland, Belgium and Norway as well as France had fallen to the Germans, and the Italians had invaded Greece and Egypt. Egypt was a British stronghold, the pivot upon which depended the grip of the Allied forces upon North Africa and the Middle East, and their eventual ability to pierce the German defences on the under side of Europe. What Malta and Gibraltar were to the Mediterranean Fleet, Egypt was to the land forces. In terms of turnover it was Naafi's largest overseas base, under command of the Headquarters Supervisor Middle East, Colonel (later Brigadier) H. Tatlow. The headquarters building in Cairo housed a waxworks on the ground floor (not a Naafi enterprise) and the populace, enjoying their local Tussauds, were unaware that a group of men upstairs had the responsibility of planning and buying provisions for armies spread over some two thousand miles of territory in North Africa and the Middle East.

The fluctuating fortunes of war, from Wavell's advance in December 1940 through the Western Desert as far as Benghazi, to Mont-

Bring on the dancing girls. ENSA 'concert party', Egypt, 1943

Bring on the music. Naafi entertainment branch tours the war theatres, 1942

Naafi money tokens, Egypt, 1941

At the foot of the great Giza Pyramid, some of the 100 ATS/EFI girls sent to the Middle East in 1943

gomery's resounding victory over Rommel at El Alamein at the end of 1942 have been fully documented and need no retelling, but the contribution of Naafi has had no place in the official histories. It is a story of shortages made good by improvisation, of hardship and losses, of swift movement and siege, of surviving defeat and keeping pace with victory. Early in the North African campaigns, staging areas were set up at 100-mile intervals westwards from Alexandria, each of which might have three or four bulk issue stores and a number of roadhouses. Supplies came either by the single line railway from Alexandria or, beyond Mersa Matruh where the rail ended, by sea into the small ports of Egypt and Libya. Inland from the coast road was the Sahara, in whose trackless wastes the war looked like a naval battle with tanks for ships.

Naafi followed the troops with essential supplies (tinned food, soap, tooth and shaving gear, cigarettes, matches, biscuits, chocolate and beer), which often had to be dumped on the bare sand with only a barbed wire fence to deter looters and a tarpaulin to keep off the sun. In circumstances of sudden retreat and shortage of transport the dumps often had to be blown up and a fresh start made elsewhere. Naafi people hated to waste good food. During one North African retreat a Naafi manager, reluctant to let the enemy enjoy his store of eggs, slung a tin bath full of water between two posts, lit a fire underneath, and handed hard-boiled eggs to the troops as they passed.

In the towns, Mersa Matruh, Tobruk, Benghazi, Naafi requisitioned buildings and established breweries and bakeries. As the military position became more stable, tented supplies in the remote locations were replaced with more substantial premises. The necessary labour emerged from the desert by what seemed like spontaneous generation. An army unit would encamp in a stretch of land without any sign of other life or human habitation. Suddenly, like a mirage but without the illusion, a band of as many as 100 Bedouin would appear, willing to act as bearers in return for standard rations and pay, which they carried around in tobacco boxes. They would help to collect wood and corrugated iron and load it on lorries to provide a solid structure for the Naafi oasis. Later, when the desert war had turned in Britain's favour, Italian prisoners undertook these labours. They shared the life of their captors and were allowed to move about freely. Unlike the Bedouin, they had nowhere else to go.

The troops were much more dependent upon Naafi in the desert than in populous Europe, and some of the permanent roadhouses, such as the Ship Inn at Mersa Matruh, the Two Bees at Buq Buq,

and the Noah's Ark at El Daba, were widely known and appreciated.
The manager was ingenious in finding ways of making them attractive. He lined the walls of the Ship Inn with wicker work taken from
German shell containers, cut out the porthole glasses from wrecks
in the harbour to adorn his windows, and enhanced the nautical
effect with festoons of white rope; made tables out of barrels and
ashtrays from shell cases which were screwed to the tables to save
them from marauders.

Furnishing was often more of a problem to Naafi than getting
premises or supplies. Tatlow and Peters secured fifty tons of railway
sleepers from which their own men made chair frames and tables.
Local supplies of cane for chair bottoms became a black market
item at exorbitant prices, and Naafi beat the profiteers by shipping
cane from India. The ingenuity of some of its men would have won
them first prize in a survival exercise. They melted broken glass and
made plates, cups and saucers. When tumblers became scarce through
breakage and pilferage they improvised replacements by cutting the
tops off beer bottles and smoothing the rims.

The appreciation of the customers, including well known generals,
Ensa celebrities and visiting journalists, was recorded in hundreds of
entries in the roadhouse logbooks; formal and slangy, humorous
and stilted, in verse and prose, and in a dozen languages including
Maori. Some of the simplest were the most revealing: 'Tea always
hot', 'Even flowers on the table', 'I do hope this Naafi never moves
while I have to travel this ruddy road'. Naturally, there were a few
complaints, the most frequent being lack of 'alk', ie alcohol.

A man could raise as big a thirst west of Suez as Kipling found
to the east, but beer was low on the list of priorities for shipment. A
general improvement came when Winston Churchill, visiting the
Italian battlefields in August 1944, found that the beer allocation
was only one quart bottle per head per week, and gave orders to step
up the supply in all theatres to three quarts a week. Though still
by no means lavish, this meant that, in addition to local production
in the Middle East and Italy, thirty million bottles a month had to be
shipped from home and distributed overseas.

Many of Naafi's customers were less surprised at the occasional
absence of alcohol than at its availability in the most unlikely places.
Group Captain F. S. Wakeham, one of the three Service members
of the board in 1962, has said: 'Towards the end of 1940 I travelled
by the Nile Valley to Khartoum, and I shall always remember
arriving at an extremely hot and isolated place called Shellal with a
number of very thirsty airmen . . . Imagine our surprise when we

discovered a Naafi selling ice-cool beer from a tent erected on a patch of sand! Until that time I must admit I had not bothered to enquire much about Naafi, and in common with many of my colleagues of those days was generally very ignorant about the whole organisation.'

Troops under siege in the towns were often less fortunate. In 1941 an Allied force held out for eight months in Tobruk, and immobilised enemy forces till relief came in the counter attack from Egyptian territory. Naafi's needs were signalled to its headquarters in Cairo, and as usual it had to put up with broken stowage. Supply ships small enough to enter Tobruk harbour were liable to be sunk by enemy gunfire, and therefore destroyers took over, anchoring well off shore and offloading on to lighters. Where Naafi's consignments fell short they could sometimes be made good by barter; for instance, a whisky surplus would be exchanged for the Australian garrison's excess chocolate. When short of drinking water, the garrison made stills out of petrol cans and distilled sea water.

At Christmas time Naafi made a great effort to ensure that every unit in North Africa had the traditional fare. All hands, including the accounting staff, were mobilised to man the convoys. A month before Christmas 1944, Naafi sent out a camel convoy from Benghazi with Christmas puddings, tinned chicken and mincemeat for a unit stationed in a lonely oasis 600 miles away in the Libyan Desert. The journey took three weeks and there were only two oases to halt at on the way.

The fascination of desert lands, reported by so many travellers, is confirmed by Naafi executives now at the Imperial Court headquarters, who bore the heat, sandstorms and bombing at Saharan roadhouses during their wartime service, and still feel nostalgia for those tough yet exhilarating times. They did not envy their colleagues on softer assignments in Bermuda and Jamaica; or in Iceland, where fires were kept blazing day and night in the stores to prevent the beer from freezing and bursting the bottles; or those east of Suez in Persia and Iraq, helping to maintain an overland supply route to Russia in conditions that alternated between intense heat and bitter cold.

The army in Persia and Iraq (Paiforce) was more than a feeder for the Russian campaigns; it was an operational force keyed for action if the enemy should strike southwards to the Persian Gulf. The pre-war Naafi installation serving the RAF at Habbaniya in Iraq had to be expanded rapidly to meet the needs of Force HQ in Baghdad, a Corps HQ and various formations in the field. In addition to bulk stores and junior ranks' canteens, it operated a number of officers' clubs in both countries and a rail-borne bulk store plying regularly between Ahwaz and Teheran. Supplies in the main came through Basra but some were brought across the Syrian desert from Damascus, and bottled beer – ten wagonloads a day – was loaded at Aleppo and carried by rail to Mosul and Baghdad. Ten wagonloads of empties returned daily by the same route.

From June 1941, in Syria and Lebanon, Naafi served the British 9th Army and elements of the RAF in Beirut, Tripoli, Damascus and other centres stretching from Aleppo to the borders of Palestine. Canteens, bulk stores, officers' clubs and a very popular beach leave centre at Beirut did thriving business in relatively peaceful conditions, while 9th Army watched political events and ensured stability in an area where famine had caused chaos and thousands of deaths in the 1914-18 war.

Even in the Levant, life for Naafi was not all roses, for in early summer 1945 fighting broke out between the Free French and the Syrians, and the EFI officers' club in Damascus, caught between the opposing forces, had to be evacuated. Some months later the Army and Naafi moved completely to Lebanon.

While the 8th Army was pursuing the beaten enemy westward from El Alamein, the British 1st Army and an American force had invaded French North Africa and advanced through Algeria and Tunisia to complete the occupation of the African side of the Mediterranean. The campaign brought some harrowing moments to Naafi employees. The driver of a mobile canteen, turning off a road to park, heard shouts from his comrades and learnt that he had plunged 100 yards through a minefield. He returned in his own tracks without mishap. A more complicated adventure befell Mr Cyril Shurmer, now on the headquarters staff at Imperial Court. He had to visit a fruit farm to arrange a large consignment of oranges for Naafi, and procured the temporary release under escort of the farm's owner, who had been jailed on suspicion (erroneous as it happened) of having been implicated in the assassination of the Vichy French leader Admiral Darlan. On the return journey the car crashed on a mountain road, fell thirty feet, and only Mr Shurmer of the party of four escaped serious injury. He did not, however, escape police questioning, from which he was rescued by an English lady missionary. All the victims survived, the prisoner established his innocence, and Naafi got its dearly bought oranges.

It was during the campaign in north-west Africa that Naafi began to extend its services to include social amenities for the men as well as meals, refreshments and personal shopping. Naafi had some officers' clubs and canteens for other ranks, but clubs for the other ranks were being run by voluntary bodies. Divided control, however competent on each side, is always anomalous, and becomes more difficult as the functions involved expand. Not until half way through the war was it officially decided that Naafi should, logically, also organise and run Services clubs. Naafi could not muster from inside its ranks enough people skilled in social work to handle the necessary expansion. The problem was solved when Mr Royle met the Dowager Marchioness of Reading, who was chairman of the Women's Voluntary Service. She generously offered the services of WVS members to organise the social and recreational life of some of the clubs, first in North Africa and Italy, and before long in every centre from Orkney to Hong Kong.

At the club a man could get a bath and a shave, have his shoes shined, his socks darned and a loose button sewn on, get newspapers and library books, enjoy a dance or a cabaret, play billiards and table tennis, join a discussion group, see a film, and attend religious services, in addition, of course, to getting meals and snacks. In the UK, club premises were specially built or adapted, and overseas, more often than not, they were requisitioned. In Mr E. M. Joseph Naafi had a highly accomplished architect, who had served the Navy and Army Canteen Board in a similar capacity in the first world war, and had been adviser to Naafi from its foundation to his appointment as head of its works and buildings branch in August 1941. In peacetime the department, known then as the premises branch, was presided over by an official entitled Inspector of Premises. Among those who handled the job overseas was Mr W. F. Lamb, who had an almost legendary reputation for moving up with the forward troops and risking his life to locate the best premises and claim them for Naafi.

The most spectacular Naafi Club, described by the Director of Army Welfare Services in Italy as 'the finest soldiers' club in the world', was housed in Prince Umberto's palace in Naples. The building had been for three centuries the home of the rulers of Naples and the Kingdom of the Sicilies, had an art gallery, a gymnasium and a room where 1,300 could dine at a sitting. Never have 'other ranks' been so indulged. That, however, was in June 1944, when Rome had fallen to the Allies and the Italians, beaten into submission, were fighting on the side of their former enemies. The earlier phases of the campaign, the invasion of Sicily from North Africa and the long and painful slogging up the boot of Italy, were accompanied by the makeshifts and hazards familiar on other fronts. Naafi teams sometimes went ahead of the main forces and got a semblance of a canteen organised out of chaos. When they first arrived in Naples in 1943 they took over a bazaar, put in a cooking stove which they had dug out of the wreckage of a hotel, and had a meal ready for the approaching troops. As in North Africa, Naafi recruited local labour. One of the most vivid memories of the war in Italy is the sight of a handful of British girls, unable to speak a word of Italian, dragooning two thousand Italian men unable to understand a word of English.

Naafi helped to bring normal life back to Italy, restoring opera houses, hotels and restaurants. Its commanders got brewmasters released from the Italian and British armies to start up the breweries, imported hops, and had the first mould of yeast flown over from England. Its descendants are probably continuing the good work in Italy to this day.

With the liberation, first of Italy and next of France, and total victory in prospect, Naafi was able to extend the range of supplies beyond the strict necessities, to provide the means of recreation and amusement behind the lines in the occupied territories. These included the more bulky sports equipment and musical instruments for the dance bands. Most of the instruments were bought second-hand and the source was rapidly drying up, but with the help of the Board of Trade and the Association of Musical Instrument Manufacturers, standardised drum sets and wood and brass instruments were made available. Austerity was lightened in other directions. Through Naafi, troops could send flowers home, and enjoy a better selection of toilet goods than the basic soaps and shaving cream. Through one of the absurdities of wartime rulings they were able to buy silk stockings for wives and girl friends but not from Naafi. Local merchants could import the stockings from the UK and sell them to the troops at ten times the price they would have had to pay if Naafi had been allowed a supply.

Experience gained in North Africa and Italy stood Naafi in good stead in the greatest trial of all, the landing of the Allied armies in Normandy on D-Day, 6th June 1944. This was the biggest seaborne invasion in the history of warfare, and the beginning of the end of Hitler's mastery in Europe. More than half a million troops had landed in a little over a week, a million within a month, and by the end of August more than two million men, three million tons of stores and four hundred thousand vehicles.

For many weeks before D-Day, troops were moved to concentration areas in the south and south-east of England, and Naafi moved with them, closing down canteens in the north and north Midlands, transporting supplies and equipment by road and rail in such a way as not to impede the movement of troops and munitions. Canteens were set up in tents, and each of the larger camps had an entertainments tent where Naafi organised parties, games and competitions, and Ensa put on concerts and variety shows. The troops needed some relaxation: the camps were sealed, no one could enter or leave without special permission, correspondence was censored, and conditions were in some respects like those of a prison camp, except that this was imprisonment in the cause of liberation.

Three thousand girls volunteered to staff the canteens, though they knew it meant isolation and primitive living. It was primitive indeed. In the chilly spring of 1944 they clumped through the mud in clogs, and when off duty huddled round stoves in portable rest huts. Many worked under artificial light all day, in tents concealed from enemy aircraft among the woodland trees. Bombing was heavy in spite of camouflage. Yet morale remained high; in fact, the girls clamoured to be allowed to land with the invasion forces. Even more remarkable was the maintenance of secrecy. Hundreds of thousands of people of both sexes knew the purpose of the build up, but nothing leaked to the enemy.

There could well have been a leakage from the supply side. As D-Day approached, Naafi warehouses were full to overflowing, and after the landings shipments were at the rate of a thousand tons a week. As canteens could not be opened till a bridgehead had been consolidated it was decided to issue special 'Naafi packs' for the crews of the small craft and for the land and air forces taking part in the invasion. The packs contained cigarettes, tobacco, cigarette papers and matches; toothpaste, shaving soap, toilet soap and razor blades; cubes of meat extract, cocoa, milk tablets and chewing gum; letter cards and pencils. In addition, immediately before embarkation, a week's supply of canteen goods was made available to the troops. The preparation of this material presented the most severe test of security. If the enemy's intelligence service had discovered the number of packs it could have gauged the numerical strength of the invasion forces.

These emergency supplies could not be treated as an ordinary commercial transaction. There was no time for the presentation of accounts and the collection of money. Lieutenant-Colonel H. P. T. Prideaux, negotiating with Naafi on behalf of 21 Army Group, suggested supplying the packs on credit and Naafi agreed, seconding

an executive to follow the customer into the field. There may have
been cases of creditors who have travelled as far, but there can be
few who lived for six months with an advancing army and shared its
battles. By the time the account was settled a large part of France
and the whole of Belgium had been liberated.

The planning of Naafi's part in the invasion of Europe had been
handled by that sturdy veteran, Brigadier W. N. Hamilton, who had
led Naafi so successfully in North Africa. His second in command
was Major W. F. Beale, back from the Naafi command in West
Africa. Every morning during the planning months they conferred
with Major-General R. G. (later Sir Randle) Feilden, at that time
Deputy Quarter-Master-General 21 Army Group. Their headquarters
was in St Paul's School, London, till August when it was moved to
Bayeux. Another veteran of the Western Desert campaigns, Brigadier
Norman Peters, MC, led the first Naafi contingent to Normandy.
It was the fulfilment of an ambition cherished for nearly five years,
since he had had the privilege of being first across the Channel in
1939.

In some respects Naafi's task was easier than it had been in earlier
campaigns. Its leaders and the commanders in the field had learnt
some lessons in co-operation and organisation from Egypt and
North Africa, and the improved relationship was reflected in the
canteen and club services. There was also the stimulus of following a
victorious army. From June 1944 till the end of the war in Europe
Naafi was free from the agony of having to abandon buildings and
stores, grab the cash box from under the enemy's nose, scrounge a
lorry from troops in retreat who felt, perhaps with some reason, that
their own need was the greater, and then start afresh, in some battered no-man's-land, to find a building, assemble some furniture and
provide pot luck for fighting men even more tired and hungry than
themselves. The prevailing optimism had even loosened slightly the
official grip on food and materials, and Naafi was able to cater more
generously and imaginatively for the troops. The canteen pack supplied for the initial wave of the invasion was followed within a few
weeks by a sports pack, weighing only 36lb and fitted with handles,
containing football cases and bladders, dartboard, draughts, domino
and cribbage outfits, packs of cards, books, and the ubiquitous army
game known at that time as lotto, but in the earlier world war as
housey-housey, and today famous (or notorious according to one's
point of view) as bingo.

Three days after the advance party had landed on a Normandy
beach the first stores were unloaded, and by 1st July Naafi opened

its first base canteen depot at Sully. A fortnight later it had two base canteens, eight bulk stores, and two mobile canteens (increasing to eighteen by the end of July) in operation. Meanwhile a bar had been fixed up in Caen and a brewery taken over nearby. The Naval Canteen Service played a vital part in the D-Day landings. Naafi boats under continual fire carried supplies to hundreds of Royal Navy ships which had no canteens. In some of the troop carriers the canteen remained open day and night for weeks, and the staff, in addition to their ordinary duties, carried out first aid during action stations. The NCS had also made provision for parties recalled from or wounded in the assault on the beaches, by equipping four accommodation ships, which stood off the Normandy coast ready to offer full canteen facilities.

The speed of the Allied advance from Normandy often brought Naafi some unaccustomed tasks. A mobile canteen which had lost its way and entered the Belgian town of St Vincent ahead of the foremost troops, was mistaken for an armoured car of the resistance movement and liberated six Allied airmen hiding in a cellar. Another mobile received the surrender of some German soldiers, and delivered them to a prisoners of war camp along with the provisions.

As Northern France and Belgium fell before the onslaught, canteens and garrison clubs sprang up in the ports and cities. When Brussels was taken on 3rd September 1944, the EFI headquarters were moved to that city from Sully and remained there until transferred to Germany soon after the war in Europe. Naafi found sumptuous premises for its seven other ranks' clubs in France and Belgium. The Montgomery Club in Brussels, named after the victor of Alamein, was the largest in Europe. The Twenty-One Dance Club in Brussels, accommodating more than three thousand people, was one of several dance halls established with the help, in an honorary capacity, of Mr (now Sir Billy) Butlin, well known as a pioneer of holiday camps in Britain.

By the end of the war in Europe, officially on 8th May 1945, Naafi had overseas 23 residential and 36 non-residential officers' clubs, 19 clubs for warrant officers and sergeants, and 68 clubs for other ranks. Additional to these were the hostels run partly by Naafi and partly by philanthropic bodies. These were hotels taken over by the Army where officers and other ranks could stay on a forty-eight hours' compulsory leave. Naafi clubs came later in the UK than on the Continent, but as the fighting ceased they helped to relieve the tedium for a vast influx of repatriated troops, liberated prisoners and Allied forces on the way home. For troops in transit Naafi also organised buffet cars on leave trains, supplied from depots set up at large railway stations and ports. Naafi employed 300 to 400 people on this service.

That troops need to be entertained as well as fed, clothed and housed, was one of the lessons that Naafi had learnt from the experience of its predecessors in the first world war. From its birth in 1921, it had had an entertainment branch which provided concerts and variety shows for camps and barracks in the more isolated posts at home and overseas. When war loomed in 1938, Mr Basil Dean, well known entrepreneur and producer and a pioneer of army entertainment as a young officer in the first world war, mobilised a team of volunteers among his show business friends to cooperate with Naafi in organising Forces' entertainment. This organisation laboured under the official title of Entertainments National Service Association. It was about as inspiring a label as Navy, Army and Air Force Institutes and of course was similarly abbreviated. For every thousand people who know it by its appropriately jaunty name of Ensa, there can hardly be one who can say what the letters stand for. At the start of the second world war Ensa became closely associated with the entertainment branch of Naafi. Mr Dean was appointed Naafi's full time director of entertainments and the whole activity was designated the Department of National Service Entertainment.

Eight days after the declaration of war, Naafi took over the Theatre Royal, Drury Lane, as its entertainment branch and Ensa headquarters. By Christmas 1939 Ensa was giving a thousand shows a week in the UK alone, and by April of the following year its total audience had grown to three million. Ensa went everywhere: to Gibraltar, Malta, Italy, the Western Desert and the Middle East, to East and West Africa, to Aden, India and Ceylon, to the Faroes and Iceland and to remote outposts such as the Cocos Islands. They suffered bombing and shelling with the troops, but in good theatrical tradition the show went on. In some places Ensa performances were watched with awe, amazement and finally delight, by people who had never seen a modern sophisticated show. This happened not only in remote regions of Africa but also in our own Shetlands. 'The social event of the week', says *Roof Over Britain*, the official story of the anti-aircraft defences in the first half of the war, 'was the visit of an Ensa film unit. It was a godsend to everybody. The apparatus was rigged up in a hut, and the shows were open to the Shetlanders. They came from miles around, by every possible means of conveyance except Shetland ponies, of which there seemed to be very few.

Many of the Islanders had never seen a film before and never seen a train. Afterwards they would push back the benches, sprinkle French chalk on the floor, and dance to music from the film unit's sound apparatus.'

To name all the famous stars who gave performances for nominal fees under the Ensa banner in every naval, military and air force station, would fill pages. They included Gracie Fields, Vera Lynn, Will Fyffe, Leslie Henson, George Robey, George Formby, Arthur Askey, Flanagan and Allen, Beatrice Lilley, Bebe Daniels, Josephine Baker, the Western Brothers, Vivien Leigh, Richard Tauber, Alice Delysia, Geraldo, Moiseiwitch and Sir Adrian Boult. Allied troops were entertained by many of their own artists, exiled like themselves from France, Belgium, Czechoslovakia, Norway. Some of them had escaped through the net of the enemy's occupying forces, or by devious ways through neutral countries; a Norwegian baritone had crossed from Norway to Scotland in an open boat. Naafi had to accommodate the Ensa artists in hostels, and also provide special kinds of transport; not only coaches to carry the performers, but lorries for stage sets and props, workshop lorries, mobile cinema vans, and vans for the 'sing-song' parties known as 'Ensatainments'. Naafi trained girls as cinema projectionists, and provided military training for entertainment officers because they had to wear the RASC/EFI uniform and assume a military character when serving overseas.

By 1944 there were 4,000 artistes on the Naafi payroll. In one month Ensa put on 13,500 stage shows and 20,000 film shows at a cost of £450,000. The service had spread to factory workers as well as the armed forces. Through Ensa Naafi had gone into show business in a big way. There were heart searchings on the Naafi board. Of all its services to the troops, this one was the most difficult to evaluate and control. Like other morale raisers its value had, to some extent, to be taken on trust. But there were no doubts among the audiences. They welcomed Ensa with the greatest enthusiasm, counting the days to the next show. War can be boring as well as over-stimulating, and nerves can be as severely tried behind the lines as under continual bombardment. There was no adequate alternative to Ensa as a nerve tonic. But the Naafi management, who had to foot the bill, suffered much anxiety over the mounting cost. Naafi had agreed with the Treasury to limit the cost of entertainment to a million pounds a year, but as it mounted far beyond that figure a new arrangement became necessary. The Treasury undertook to support the activity by means of cash advances and by leaving on

loan to Naafi certain funds which would otherwise have been paid
to the State, while Naafi was to reimburse the Treasury to the extent
of sixty per cent of whatever profit the Corporation had accumulated
by the end of the war. The Treasury also agreed to the appointment
of Marshal of the Royal Air Force Sir Edward Ellington as controller of entertainment at Naafi to act as liaison with government
departments and generally to supervise the entertainment side of
Naafi. The total cost to Naafi of Ensa's wartime shows was about
£17 million.

Naafi's losses during the war as well as costs had been formidable.
The fall of France and Norway had lost Naafi nearly £1,400,000,
and further big trading losses resulted from military reverses in the
Western Desert and withdrawals from Greece, Crete and Far
Eastern territories. But Naafi's profitable trading more than outweighed the losses and all debts were repaid in full, partly from the
realisation of stocks when the war was over. Among the debts was
over £10 million owing to the Treasury. On 23rd October 1947 the
Corporation handed to the Treasury a cheque for £10,500,000.

As a feat of management Naafi's post-war solvency was even more
impressive than it appears. Apart from the provision of premises
which had always been covered out of the public purse, Naafi's
service to the armed forces had not cost the State a penny. It was not
only the State that benefited. Out of its surpluses Naafi had made
grants to the Service benevolent or welfare funds, which helped to
build up the healthy capital position they enjoy to this day. The
customers had also had more immediate concessions in the form of
large price reductions, free sports goods, newspapers and periodicals.

Management is one of the invisibles of business: it is known by its
results; and the management of Naafi, which had no shareholders
except the three Services, was less visible than its counterparts in normal business. During the war it had to buy as judiciously as the shortage of supplies and urgency of demand permitted. It had to salvage
what it could out of disasters beyond its control. It had to watch over
its consumable and durable goods in dozens of lands and on every sea,
in locations where no ordinary trader would choose to operate, and
in circumstances where property was at the mercy of tip and run
marauders who could not always be stopped and could rarely be
prosecuted. Naafi's investigation branch, presided over as from
June 1941 by an ex-police officer Mr O. Quinn, lent to Naafi by
Aspro Limited, operated in all parts of the world. Considering the
temptations and opportunities, the motley local manpower employed, and the vagaries of defeat and victory, Naafi proved to be a

remarkably good insurance risk. The total amount recovered from the insurance companies during the whole war was about £450,000, while the premiums paid in one year alone, 1944-5, amounted to £330,000.

The lack of precision in the definition of Naafi status, rights and functions added to the burden of the top management. A clearly written official brief, based perhaps on a modified Draper Report, would have forestalled many problems which took months and in some cases years to resolve. For instance, there comes a time in the life of a 'harumfrodite' when it has to be classified as one thing or the other. Naafi personnel were paid by Naafi as civilians but, attached to the RASC or the ATS in the field, they came under military discipline. Could they therefore have their pay docked like soldiers as punishment for certain offences? And how, and how much, would members of RASC proper be paid when lent to Naafi to help with the canteen services? It took the Army nearly two years to find a formula for these difficulties. In addition, the pay of Naafi employees who had to be commissioned and enlisted for operational duties, had to be reconciled to the satisfaction of both sides with that of the corresponding ranks in the Army, and their income tax position had also to be made clear.

Pricing of goods was another problem tangled with complications. Naafi's policy of keeping its prices level with those charged by local shops was complicated in Egypt and other Middle Eastern countries by a long-standing arrangement granting the British Forces immunity from customs duties on imported goods, and this tended to undercut the local trade. The Egyptian government had insisted that the value of the duty should be passed on to the troops. In order to prevent such goods, especially cigarettes, from getting into the black market and upsetting the local economy, Naafi was persuaded not to reduce the prices of those goods by the full amount of duty escaped, but agreed with the Army that the extra profit so made should be used to reduce the price of other goods (tea, ice cream and minerals) by an equivalent amount. The ordinary customer did not always understand the complexity of Naafi's pricing problems, but Naafi did in time win due appreciation, and was even called upon to help in emergencies outside the range of its responsibilities. When Army units had difficulty with their messing supplies they were glad to arrange supplies through Naafi's highly organised buying department.

Sometimes the demands on Naafi's services were excessive, but that is one of the penalties of success. When the troops leap-frogged from North Africa to Sicily and then to Italy they asked Naafi for a build up of amenities in Italy which would have required a great increase in Naafi manpower and strained the Corporation's finances. The financial control on the board of management had to decide where to draw the line. An unusual request came from the Royal Navy when victory in Europe was assured and Britain had started to build up her forces in the Far East for the liberation of Malaya, Singapore and the Dutch East Indies from Japanese occupation. Since the Navy would be operating far from a major base, it asked for two large merchant ships to be fitted up at a cost of £750,000 each as floating clubs, complete with shops, cafeterias, ice cream and soda fountains, saloon bars, barbers' shops, shoe repairer, tailor and bookstalls, and offering facilities for a thousand men a day on each ship. The most original feature was to have been a fully equipped brewery in each ship capable of producing 250 barrels of beer a week. One ship actually went into production, and gave its customers a chance to discover what beer tasted like made with water distilled from the sea instead of drawn from the delectable springs of Burton on Trent. But the experiment was short-lived, because Japanese resistance collapsed before the project was completed.

These ships were to have been an element in what was expected to be a prolonged campaign against the Japanese in South-East Asia. After the fall of Malaya, Singapore and Hong Kong, Naafi had disappeared from the Far Eastern theatre except for its canteens in ships of the Royal Navy. Their contribution has received a deserved but all too rare tribute in Mr John Winton's book *The Forgotten Fleet*. 'It appears that Naafi had a grasp of military strategy at least as good as that of the Combined Chiefs of Staff. They were apparently never in any doubt that a British Fleet would operate in the Pacific, for as early as October 1943 their agents in Fremantle were instructed to rent a warehouse, and the following February a Naval Canteen Service representative, Commander G. H. Rogers, RNVR [now Naafi's regional manager, Aldershot], was dispatched from the Middle East to Australia as Naafi representative. By the end of the war there were Naafi warehouses at Fremantle, Sydney, Melbourne and Brisbane, and at thirty-one shore establishments. There were four Naafi canteens in the Admiralty Islands. The BPF was perhaps Naafi's biggest challenge of the war; never had Naafi been asked to provide for such numbers of Naafi stores as they were asked to do, through the medium of the Fleet Train, to the ships of the British Pacific Fleet.' He describes how Naafi kept the fleet supplied in spite of dock strikes and shortages of boats and equipment, and how the members of the Naval Canteen Service 'took a full part in the operational life of their ships, sharing the same hardships and discomforts, and, at action stations, serving in stretcher parties, ammunition handling parties, and as navigational plotters'.

It was not till quite late in the war that Naafi again became shore-based in the East. The Indian Canteen Corps had served the mixed Allied Forces throughout the campaign against the Japanese invaders in Burma. Towards the end of 1944 the Corps, acutely short of officers, asked Naafi for help, and Naafi, though in similar difficulties, lent them nineteen officers. When the tide of battle had turned in Burma and the Allies were advancing southwards towards Rangoon, they were being supplied by air drop from a large depot in Chittagong in charge of a Naafi officer.

Meanwhile large depots were being organised in Ceylon and at Madras for the recovery of Britain's South-East Asian dependencies. In command of the Naafi operation was Colonel C. A. Layard (today merchandise director on the Naafi board of management); he was attached to the headquarters of the Supreme Allied Commander, South-East Asia, then Admiral Lord Louis Mountbatten. Colonel Layard created a planning and operational headquarters in Kandy to build up resources of men, equipment and supplies for the invasion of Malaya and Singapore. The lessons of the earlier war years had by now been fully learnt, and Naafi had all the co-operation it needed from the commanders in the field. It attended planning meetings for the allocation of shipping space and warehousing. Its leader was shown aerial photographs of enemy-occupied Singapore so that he could stake a claim to premises. Landing craft full of men and stores were ready to sail when the atomic bombing of Hiroshima and Nagasaki brought the war to an abrupt end. Naafi had to redeploy its resources overnight to occupational forces in territories stretching from Java to Japan. But that was only one of many problems that were to confront the Corporation in the troubled peace that followed.

CHAPTER FOUR

The Troubled Peace

During the second world war Naafi's main structural problem had been how to grow enormously without bursting. After the war the problem was how to shrink without collapsing. For Naafi, unlike private business and nationalised industries, growth could never be a policy but only a matter of expediency. Naafi grows and diminishes with the armed forces. If Britain decided to double her military and naval strength Naafi would double in size. If Britain disarmed completely Naafi would be wound up. It is run as a business, but is contained within a straitjacket. The only comparable enterprise is the Royal Ordnance Factories, which manufacture armaments for the Forces; but they have some leeway which Naafi is not allowed. With government consent they can supply military vehicles and weapons to other countries and even use some spare capacity in producing industrial and consumer durables for private companies. They differ also in being a department of the Ministry of Defence, instead of in a limbo between the public and the private sectors.

The shrinking process was not precipitate or evenly distributed: the momentum of war prolongs many activities far past the cease fire date. In some places the shut down was immediate. On 9th May 1945, the day after the official end of the war in Europe, the commander of the fleet based on Scapa Flow told Naafi's area manager that he could disperse, and the entire fleet sailed immediately for Australian waters. The area manager, suddenly deprived of all his customers, began closing canteens almost daily.

In another area, however, facing Scapa across the North Sea, Naafi actually had to start up a service, establishing bulk issue stores and mobile canteens for 70,000 liberated Norwegian prisoners of war. In all theatres of war, Naafi helped to repatriate prisoners, many of them Naafi employees. Some of the most pitiful cases were survivors of the Japanese prisoners of war camps and of the notorious 'death railway' built by forced labour on the Siam-Burma border – emaciated, exhausted by dysentery and malaria, and half blind

'Noah's Ark.' *A tented canteen in the Western Desert,*
North Africa, 1942

The D-Day invasion: the 13th and 18th Hussars land on
'White Beach' – one of the code names used for the landing areas,
Normandy, 6th June 1944

British troops and a Sherman tank pass through a devastated village, Normandy, 1944

through malnutrition. When Hong Kong was overrun by the Japanese and the garrison imprisoned, a Naafi master baker smuggled seven pounds of yeast into the camp, fed and developed it with hot rice water and sugar, and for three months, undetected by his captors, was able to supplement his own and his fellow prisoners' diet of rice, chrysanthemum leaves and parsnips with a daily eggcup-full of yeast water.

Troops going home, as well as released prisoners, needed looking after, and without Naafi canteens, clubs and packs many of them would have found their first few days of freedom bleak indeed. Naafi took over where the command left off and a vast floating clientele kept the Institutes busy at home and overseas. Though the bulk of the EFI reverted to civilian status, they had to stay in some areas where fighting continued or new conflicts had arisen. In other places Naafi's job was redeployment rather than closing down; canteens and clubs were opened in occupied Germany as they closed in France and Italy, and the North African units fell back upon Egypt as the centre for Army and Naafi action in the turbulent Middle East. In the years following the capitulation of Japan on 15th August 1945 and the final end of the second world war, there was hardly a month when Britain's armed forces were not under attack or quelling strife somewhere in the world, and Naafi at their elbows with appropriate refreshment and recreation. The wars in this period of troubled peace, and Naafi's contribution, will be described later.

At the same time, Naafi had to maintain its viability as a business, disposing of all stock at not too great a loss and buying judiciously in a post-war economy beset with material shortages, rationing and currency restrictions. Some of the privileges that Naafi had enjoyed during the national emergency were now withdrawn. The buying department could no longer apply for dollars to buy biscuits and chocolate in hard currency areas, but had to queue up along with other claimants in a deprived home market. There were fewer top priorities for fighting men who were not actually fighting.

That was not to say that Naafi would revert to its pre-war stan-dards. The troops had returned to temporary austerity and a nation suffering under the burden of a costly victory, but a new world was sprouting from the debris. Post-war demands from the armed forces would be more exacting than between the wars. Recruitment was going to be more difficult and the path would need to be smoothed with better pay and service conditions. Naafi too would have a recruitment problem for the generally unexciting duties of peace,

F

though it could still offer tempting and tough assignments overseas. Improved employee relations were in the air throughout commerce and industry, and Naafi would have to follow the trend.

Amid these considerations Naafi had to remember one of the fundamental clauses in its articles of association, the obligation to maintain 'the nucleus of a service capable of immediate expansion on mobilisation'. The euphoria that had followed the first world war, expressed by the slogan 'a war to end war', was absent this time. While no major war was in sight, the world was too unstable politically for anyone to indulge in false optimism. Naafi intended to be ready if another war should arise. Looking back on its war record it had more cause for self-congratulation than for regret, but some important lessons emerged. The Munich warning had not been taken seriously enough. The twelve months to the outbreak of war had not been used to full advantage. Relations with officialdom should have been regularised before the shooting started. Not least, Naafi should have entered the war with men already trained to face the enemy, instead of delaying military training till Dunkirk pointed the moral of negligence.

The lessons were embodied in two documents. One was the *Book of the RASC (EFI) Depot* by Lieutenant-Colonel R. Merry, head of the Norwood training centre. It described in great detail the accommodation, facilities and duties of the depot and the routine of each department from reception to accounts and from messing to draft procedure. Though the lieutenant-colonel was well aware that a new and unpredictable era in warfare and international relations generally had begun when atomic bombs on Hiroshima and Nagasaki brought the war to an abrupt close, he has left a blueprint on which a successor could base a training programme.

The other document is a highly detailed report on Naafi's performance in the war by Mr E. H. Cherry. It was not published. The board of management decided that it was more suitable in style and content for the Corporation's archives than for general reading, though they acknowledged its honesty and accuracy. A later generation of managers would find it instructive in the same way as the record of the training department if a comparable challenge should arise in the future.

Meanwhile Naafi's board of management learnt some useful lessons from the experience of their predecessors after the first world war. Under Sir George Erskine's shrewd financial guidance, Naafi had come through with a handsome profit; but this profit was tied up in stocks which had to be converted into cash so that the debt to the Treasury could be repaid. Remembering the canteen scandals of a generation before, the Naafi board were determined that the manner of their own stock disposal would be above criticism. The Board of Trade had presented a White Paper to Parliament shortly before the end of the war on the disposal of surplus war stocks other than food, but had said that this did not apply to Naafi, who remained a free agent. Naafi appreciated the compliment but decided to play for safety by conforming voluntarily to the government's plan. The stock was sold only to government departments, to retailers for resale, and to large users such as municipal bodies, hospitals and catering establishments. There was no official inquiry this time; nor any public outcry about the disposal of the canteen millions.

That was the big rundown, when millions of pounds were realised; but Naafi is always selling off dead stock either centrally or locally to clear space and help to pay for modernisation. The goods that come to light at auctions are often surprising and the buyers even more so. One can understand people wanting tables, mattresses, dartboards, sports medals (Naafi once unloaded eight thousand of them) and even scrubbers' aprons, gravy strainers, packets of bronze hairpins and veteran pianos, but it would be interesting to know more about the purchasers of 242 empty blanco tins and fifty-four Father Christmas beards. It would be equally interesting to know which Naafi clubs had suddenly opted for clean-shaven Father Christmasses.

Overseas many of the auctions have been occasioned by the fluctuations of war. Mr Frank Soden, who had served Naafi in dozens of countries and was manager of the Overseas Canteen Service when he retired, recalls the civil war in Palestine in the late 1940s and the closing down of clubs as the British army evacuated the territory. Surplus furniture converging on Haifa was sold in large successive lots to a local dealer. His last cheque for a substantial purchase bounced, and in the confused condition of the country it proved impossible to recover the money. Seven years later Naafi sued the man in the Israeli courts and sent over Mr Soden, by then based in London, as its witness. The delinquent had good reason to marvel at the long arm of Naafi and the inexorability of justice: he was made to pay up in full, plus five years' interest at eight and a half per cent. That was not quite the end of the incident for Naafi. The Israeli government would not allow so much currency to leave the country but was willing to export its equivalent in citrus fruits. Thus it was the Naafi warehouse in Kennings Way, London, acquired a shipload of oranges and grapefruit in belated settlement of the Corporation's last operation in the Holy Land.

Shrinkage of commitments and establishments at home and over-seas was the negative side of Naafi's immediate post-war operations; the positive side was improvement of the services and the organisation. While, therefore, Naafi had to match the rundown in the defence forces, it was not scaled down proportionately. Smaller and better was the new policy. Nevertheless the reduction was dramatic and its successful accomplishment was a managerial triumph. Naafi's peak wartime strength had been 110,000 people; by the end of 1947 they had been reduced to 65,000, and ten years after the end of the war to 30,000. In that decade turnover had declined by two-thirds. The two figures taken together are revealing; a third of the turnover achieved by a quarter of the work force indicates a satisfactory rise in productivity.

Streamlining involved the whole organisation from the management downwards. Naafi was not under any official pressure to change its character though there had been unofficial suggestions that instead of being incorporated under the Companies Acts it might be incorporated by Royal Charter. The board could see no commercial advantage in such a change, though it would obviously have carried prestige. Naafi did, in fact, receive Royal patronage eventually. King George VI became its first Royal patron, and his daughter Queen Elizabeth II has continued to honour Naafi with her patronage.

The urgencies of war had placed a heavy burden on the chairman. In addition to the direction of policy, he undertook managerial duties which in a business in normal times would be handled by the chief executive, and he travelled widely in all war theatres and other territories where Naafi was active. When the process of compressing Naafi into its post-war frame was well under way, he felt he could shed some of the managerial work and concentrate on what he considered his main function, liaison with the Service ministries. In 1949 he invited Major-General R. G. (later Sir Randle) Feilden to join Naafi as general manager.

General Feilden was no stranger to Naafi. He had just retired after war service successively with the Guards Armoured Division, the Home Forces, 21 Army Group and the Rhine Army (the last three as Deputy Quarter-Master-General), and as Vice-Quarter-Master-General at the War Office from 1947 to 1949. In this last capacity he had attended the joint meetings of the Naafi council and the board of management. As a professional soldier of high rank and of about the same age as the commanders in the field, he could speak to them on equal terms and receive plain speaking on his own performance and the effectiveness of his team. He headed the five-man committee of senior executives instituted by Sir Lancelot Royle in the war, and co-ordinated their efforts in a weekly general managers' meeting.

His main contribution was to make Naafi attractive to bright young men seeking a career. Naafi had been rather like the civil service in its system of promotion by seniority. The war had shaken the system, as it did many other inhibitory traditions, but the speed with which some of the middle management people at the head-quarters had rushed back into civil jobs as soon as the end of the war offered release showed a lack of confidence in the flexibility of the promotional ladder. General Feilden believed that Naafi was missing some of the best brains because merit alone could not break the hierarchical barrier. He therefore abolished the old system in favour of the competitive principle that the best man wins, and instituted the selection board method of finding managerial talent. There was one selection board for senior posts, which he chaired himself, and another for junior posts, presided over by the manager, personnel department. Morale improved with the enlargement of opportunity.

Ideally the introduction of selection techniques should have been accompanied by a big investment in training facilities at all levels, but Naafi had to wait several years before it had its own staff college. The reasons were social and financial. Before the war, Naafi could recruit all the trained catering staff it needed in the employment market. During the war, when the armed services took the cream of the nation's manpower and womanpower and left Naafi to find whatever raw material remained, the Corporation worked wonders with makeshift training and inspired amateurism. After the war there was a shortage of good catering staff in the market, and the high turnover in the junior ranks reduced still further the standard of efficiency in the organisation. Cutting Naafi down to size, however, without wrecking the business, called for careful financial management, and among the departments that suffered was training. The wartime training centres in various parts of the country were closed down and by 1948 only Mayhurst in Woking remained, and it was able to train only thirty people at a time. When required, external services were used; some of Naafi's departmental heads, for instance, were sent to courses at the Administrative Staff College, Henley.

Plans for a training establishment were drawn up and approved by the board, but there were obstacles less easily surmounted even than finance. Steel for building was scarce and planning permission for new building other than housing was difficult to obtain. Finally

Naafi was granted permission to restore a derelict group of buildings in Totteridge, and in the summer of 1953 Totteridge Lodge admitted its first trainees. Within a year more than 2,500 people of all grades had passed through the college: canteen attendants, cooks, canteen manageresses, shop managers, superintendents and district managers. Cooks had a model kitchen equipped with every kind of stove they were likely to find in a Naafi canteen. Senior people went there for refresher courses but also to have practical experience of the work of their subordinates. Staff going overseas were briefed on the country and its currency.

Totteridge served Naafi's training needs for five years. Its closure in 1958 was dictated by a new need for economy in circumstances of special difficulty. Training was not abandoned but conducted in the field instead of at the centre. It became a centralised function again with the opening of the Wingham Training Centre at Claygate in Surrey in 1959.

Naafi's difficulties were made clear in the chairman's report and balance sheet for 1957, which showed a deficit of £375,447. For the first time in its thirty-seven years Naafi's profit was insufficient to meet all its obligations. After paying back, day by day and month by month, rebate and discounts at fixed rates totalling nearly £3 million, the account was in the red, and was balanced only by drawing upon sums set aside in previous years as a contingency reserve. This nest egg also enabled Naafi to top up its development reserve and, at the end of the year, find extra rebate for Service central welfare funds to the amount of £150,000. This was, however, some £700,000 less than the extra rebate paid the year before. The Services understood the situation and accepted the cut gracefully; but for Naafi it had been a 'rainy day' indeed.

The difficulties were caused by a series of blows which hit Naafi almost simultaneously. The biggest was the government's decision to abolish national service and reduce the strength of the armed forces from 690,000 to 375,000, which would virtually halve the number of Naafi's customers by 1962. The rundown of the forces started immediately in Germany where Naafi had to close twenty-six establishments. The loss of an exchange concession following currency reforms in Germany added heavily to Naafi's burdens; so did the final denial to Naafi of the right to retain any profit on the supply of messing goods to the Services, though the business continued to benefit from messing trade by the spread of overheads. Naafi's markets were closing down in Egypt and in West Africa, and its large commitment in Korea was coming to an end. The chain reaction of nationalism sparked off in all parts of the world by the liberating force of the allied victories in the second world war had reduced British power and influence and so curtailed the activities and revenue of Naafi. Yet out of its falling revenue Naafi had to improve its service to encourage larger sales to a better paid, more selective but numerically smaller clientele. The business would have to include more substantial goods and services than food, beverages, groceries and the odds and ends of Service purchases.

Some of Naafi's development requirements had been foreseen as far back as the Macharg-Royle committee, which had recommended the recruitment of executives from retail trade. One of these recruits had been Mr W. F. Beale, whose father at the turn of the century had founded the business with which Sir Lancelot Royle was to be associated in a larger grouping. He returned to the family business at the end of the war but was not allowed to remain long outside Naafi's ranks. When Sir Lancelot Royle began to plan his own return to normal retailing after steering Naafi through vast expansions and drastic retrenchment, and looked around for a likely successor, Mr William Beale, with the same background but ten years younger, seemed the obvious choice. In 1949 he was invited to join the board of management, though unaware that he had been chosen as heir apparent to the chairman. He succeeded Sir Lancelot Royle in 1953 and presided over the progress of the Corporation into the next decade.

The 1950s saw important adjustments and rationalisation. In 1954 the board appointed a committee of senior members of the management, under an independent chairman, the eminent accountant Sir Harold Howitt, to examine the organisation and procedures and show where economy and efficiency could be improved. As a result, weaknesses in administration were exposed and corrected, regional regrouping in the United Kingdom produced a more efficient structure, market trends were studied, and needs served and sometimes anticipated by experiments in service. The board of management was extended from seven to nine members, the additions being Sir Randle Feilden whose post as chief general manager had been upgraded to managing director, and Mr H. P. T. Prideaux as assistant managing director. Those were significant changes, a sign of business maturity. For the first time, Naafi was growing its own top management instead of seeking them outside. Mr Prideaux had been brought into the organisation by Sir Randle Feilden as personnel manager in succession to Mr H. G. Swithenbank (who had been made manager OCS) and was to become chairman of the board.

Another home grown director is the present chief executive, Mr

E. W. MacGowan, who joined the Naafi secretariat as a young
solicitor in 1939, then served successively with RASC/EFI and the
Navy, returned to Naafi after the war, became assistant secretary in
1949 and succeeded Mr Crosier as secretary in 1952. A feature of the
administrative tidying in the 1950s was the break up of the Central
Services into their logical units and the organisation of the
secretariat as a separate department. A plans and methods section
was formed to improve operational efficiency. Public relations
acquired more importance as a link throughout the scattered worldwide family, and as a means of making Naafi's activities better known
through the press and of correcting persistent misconceptions about
its functions and quality. Staff policy was enlightened and progressive.
Modern ideas on superannuation were incorporated in the pension
scheme. Assisted house purchase was added to the list of staff
benefits. Naafi had its own medical department to watch over staff
health and ensure hygiene in the canteens, kitchens and food
factories.

The aesthetic side of staff care was not overlooked. The old type
of uniform which had made the Naafi girl look like Little Orphan
Annie had undergone successive changes and was now redesigned
to look smart as well as businesslike. Could the new look have had
anything to do with the high marriage rate among Naafi girls?
A newspaper had calculated that Naafi girls married at the rate of
one every thirty-seven hours.

Naafi employees had always been more of a clan than a work force.
The 'Naafi bug', which past and present members talk about, really
does exist. It is a kind of 'old school' feeling which most industrial
companies cannot buy for love or bonuses. It is evident, of course,
in many cases of long service – Naafi is a large consumer of gold
watches; but its durability outside the organisation is even more
impressive. Whether or not they are members of the Old Comrades
Association, old Naafi hands tend to gravitate to Imperial Court
for exchange of reminiscences with former colleagues still clocking
up forty and more years of service.

The customer cannot be expected to develop the same loyalty,
but he shows his appreciation in other ways. When Naafi opened
seventeen temporary clubs in rented premises in Britain towards
the end of the second world war their popularity forced the pace of
more permanent development. The Service ministries authorised
Naafi to set aside money for a building programme which by the
mid-1950s would give the Home Forces twelve first rate town clubs.
Portsmouth was the first, opened on 31st January 1946 by the 19-

year-old heir to the throne, Princess Elizabeth. Other clubs, all for members of the three Services below commissioned rank, followed at less than yearly intervals at leading military and naval centres: Colchester, Chatham, Aldershot, Oswestry, Catterick, Bicester, Plymouth, Lincoln, Chippenham, Glasgow and Salisbury. They contained restaurants, lounges, bars and taverns, reading and writing rooms, music and television rooms, games rooms and ballrooms, and at Chatham, Catterick and Plymouth residential facilities. There was also a town club in Singapore, the Britannia, opened in 1952.

Apart from the range of amenities there was nothing standardised about the clubs; each was individual in architecture and decor, reflecting the ideas and taste of Naafi's distinguished adviser Mr E. M. Joseph and its design and furnishing teams. They varied from the sharp modernity of Catterick and the businesslike blocks in the heart of Glasgow to the Regency flavour of a curved bay at Oswestry and the long low elegance of the Salisbury club looking on to the Cathedral Close and harmonising with the beauty of the setting.

Canteens, too, were changed to fit the new type of Service man. The old image of beer slopped on the floor and initials carved in the table top was fading; indeed milk was fast becoming a more popular drink than beer. Precautions were still necessary, however. Naafi had a piano built to its own design with sloping lid to discourage parking of glasses, a brass kicking plate on each side of the pedals, and stainless cigarette-resistant keys. Noise was part of the amenity and juke boxes were installed in many canteens (the revenue helped to pay for what Naafi terms 'embellishments'). Vending machines, which had been used on a small scale during the war, began to spread, in ships as well as on shore. In fact the Naval Canteen Service had been the guinea pig for this development. These machines helped to overcome the disability of staff shortage, and the customer was glad to get his snack whenever he liked and as quickly as he could push the button. But it has taken a long time for him to get reconciled to the absence of the Naafi girl: you cannot swap banter with a machine.

Mechanisation came into the kitchen too. Many of the old-fashioned cookers were replaced with modern 'called order' equipment which enabled the customer to choose his steak and see it grilled. The equipment was mobile enough to be carried on manoeuvres. In an evacuation exercise by units in Germany, Naafi moved with the troops, setting up a complete canteen service at each stage including called order meals and even juke boxes. Rates of pay in the armed forces increased in step with sophistication in taste and Naafi had to cater for the new men. A poll held in the middle of the decade to place supper dishes in order of popularity showed steak, chips and tomatoes at the top of the list and sausages, veal and ham pie, and baked beans on toast from seven to ten places down.

Re-equipment was not achieved without a struggle, which was not always financial. Naafi could choose, but the Service ministries had to dispose, and before they would agree to a drastic kitchen overhaul they had to be persuaded of the need. It was easier for Naafi than for Whitehall to appreciate the economy of infra-red cooking.

In other respects, too, Naafi was in advance of its masters. Up to 1956 the junior ranks could buy beer but not wine from Naafi. The suggested opening of wine bars had been refused in 1948 by a standing committee for the welfare of the Forces. Particular opposition came from the WAAF officers, who said that wine would encourage extravagance among the young girls and antagonise their parents. Progress, however, proved stronger than prejudice. The Air Ministry, in eventually granting its consent, said that a CO could close down the wine bar if he saw a deterioration in behaviour. So privates, 'erks' and ratings ashore got their sherry, and members of the Women's Services shared the privilege without moral decline.

It was not until 1949 that common sense was brought to bear on the cleaning of canteens, a function in which divided control had created a situation worthy of Gilbert and Sullivan. The premises were provided by the military, naval or air force unit, but Naafi ran the canteen service. Therefore, according to King's Regulations, Naafi would clean behind the counter where none but Naafi feet had trodden, while the cleaning of the customers' side of the counter was a unit responsibility. There were one or two curious gaps in the roll of duties. For instance, for a time Naafi was responsible for cleaning the walls up to 8 feet from the floor, and the State from 12 feet upwards, but the middle segment was no one's official care. While Naafi was flexible enough to stretch across another four feet of wall space, the broader problem of divided control could not be disposed of without the consent of the Services. Naafi petitioned long, and logically, to be allowed to put out the cleaning of its premises to contract and charge up the cost. It took years for the Services to appreciate that cleaning and maintenance should be the Naafi manager's concern, that it was easier to ensure quality if the work was commissioned and paid for direct, and that in any case it was false economy to use Service men as housemaids.

In the comparatively leisurely pre-war years when the Forces had ample manpower, it was easy enough to spare men for scrubbing floors and washing windows, though these duties were far from popular. The much smaller post-war armed forces have had better things to do, and with the arrival of the military salary and the improved status that it signified, the Naafi 'fatigues' became more and more absurd. Gradually, over the years, the Services have relinquished portions of their share in control to Naafi.

Cleaning has been only one area of divided control. Others are furnishing, decoration and the provision of a long list of restaurant, club and shop equipment. The need to get the agreement and support of the Services for expenditure on the re-equipment and modernisation for which they were responsible has often been an embarrassment to Naafi and a brake on progress; and where Naafi has been permitted to use its own discretion and money it has seldom been possible to obtain full reimbursement. It is not so easy for those who hold the purse strings outside the Naafi organisation to see the need for keeping up with trade practice as keenly as Naafi's business brains. Ideally, Naafi should operate as a self-contained commercial enterprise, covering all development out of revenue; but in order to do this, the management would have to have the right to refuse unprofitable assignments, which would be unthinkable in an institution dedicated to the provision of a service wherever defence needs might dictate, irrespective of economic considerations. The Services have tried to be helpful. Within the last two or three years they have formed a Joint Services Naafi Co-ordinating Committee to save Naafi from having to negotiate separately with each department. Somehow, Naafi contrives to reconcile modern business needs with its dependence upon the Services.

Modern methods were introduced into the shops in the decade following the end of the second world war. In the UK more than 40,000 Service families shopped with Naafi, and it was becoming increasingly difficult to get reliable staff. Naafi was among the first of the British retail grocery chains to realise that the remedy was in self-service. It opened its first self-service shop at RAF Kabritt in Egypt as early as 1953, and its first in Europe at Fontainebleau in 1956. As a location Fontainebleau could not have been bettered. Service men of fifteen nations with their families were concentrated in the Paris region, attached to SHAPE (Supreme Headquarters of the Allied Powers in Europe), whose headquarters was at Rocquencourt north of Paris, and AFCENT (Allied Forces Central Europe) based on Fontainebleau; and SHAPE had invited Naafi five years before to organise a canteen service for its headquarters personnel and their dependants. Among the most appreciative of the Fontainebleau shop's international customers were the Americans, to whom self-service had long been familiar at home. Scandinavia, too, was

ahead of the UK in the application of self-service to retailing, and
it was there that senior Naafi officials studied trends before opening
self-service shops in Germany and Britain. Naafi even introduced
self-service into mobile shops. The first of these was equipped to serve
the scattered Service families at Tidworth.

The variety of goods carried by Naafi shops was surprisingly large.
The Corporation's supplies department claimed to handle about fifteen thousand saleable items, ranging from cigarette lighters to washing machines, watches to record players, fashion goods to greeting
cards, typewriters to fairy cycles, and even for one customer a yacht
(not a stock item!). Naafi was beginning to package goods under its
own name: it had its own blends of ground coffee and tea and employed tea tasters. Goods bought in bulk were tested and foodstuffs
strictly controlled. There was even a team of girl nut samplers who
rejected ten per cent as below Naafi standards. The supplies department was also responsible for supplying messing goods to many units
and to the very active special catering department which provided refreshments for the Forces at events of all sizes from a small unit party
to the Coronation of Queen Elizabeth II. The supplies department
also provided furniture and tableware to Naafi canteens. The replacement business alone was colossal. A quarter of a million cups
were broken every year in the canteens. It was estimated that seven
journeys across the counter completed the life span of a cup.

Associated with supplies was an export branch. Though Naafi
was not a trader in the ordinary commercial sense of the term, it had to
stand freight and other overseas transportation costs and had to cover
these in its prices or make a loss. Naafi prices at the point of sale were
a subject of controversy throughout the decade. The press sometimes
accused Naafi of charging higher prices for most British goods in
some remote foreign station than for the equivalent goods at home.
Some of the reports were exaggerated or due to misunderstanding.
Many of the goods in question were supplied by Naafi in bulk to
Service units who resold them on their own terms over which Naafi
had no control. After a newspaper campaign on behalf of the Forces
in Korea, Mr L. C. Wynne-Tyson, a deputy general manager, went
out to investigate, and on his return told the press why prices abroad
had to differ from those at home. Some articles, especially those such
as cigarettes and spirits, whose price in the UK was inflated by a heavy
duty, were actually cheaper in overseas countries which admitted
them duty free than they were at home, in spite of export costs;
but most others, even after deduction of purchase tax, had to bear
heavy charges which affected the price.

Naafi's pricing policy overseas is complex, and still liable to be misunderstood. It would take many pages to explain in detail. Briefly, Naafi tries overseas, as it does in the UK, to keep prices, less duty escaped, of groceries and household goods at the general level of the prevailing prices for articles of a similar kind in reputable civilian shops such as Service men and their families might patronise in the absence of Naafi. Where there are no normal shopping facilities, or where for other reasons no standard of comparison is possible, Naafi has to decide what is a reasonable price, taking into account freight, insurance, special packing, extra refrigeration where necessary, warehousing, and the cost of five or six times as much handling as consignments receive travelling between two points in the UK. Naafi has no transport privileges; it pays the cost like any other exporter. Extra protective packaging for export of vulnerable foodstuffs adds further to the cost, and containers are not recoverable from overseas. The prices charged must allow for a surplus to be returned to the Services. The Ministry of Defence accepts Naafi's pricing policy, and takes prices into account when calculating the cost of living on overseas stations for local overseas allowances.

Some critics have asked why Naafi does not cut out the rebate and reduce prices accordingly. There are two reasons: first, the decision does not rest with Naafi but with the Services, whose welfare projects and charities depend largely upon these rebates; second, if the rebate were to be spread over millions of small purchases, the benefit to the individual customer would not be apparent. On the other hand, the aggregate rebate is much more substantial than the Service men and their families realise. In its fifty years, Naafi has returned to the Services an average of about £3⅜ million a year in rebates and discounts.

Naafi's difficulties have always underlined the differences between a tied and a free enterprise. Under the heading 'Planning for the Unpredictable' Sir William Beale wrote in his report for the year 1956, 'There is no such thing as a normal Naafi year. Normality implies the usual and familiar, whereas in Naafi it is always the unusual and unfamiliar which compose the pattern of its trade. In ordinary civilian businesses – and I write with experience of the distributive trades – some measure of normality, some common factor between one trading period and another may, and indeed must, be found if forward plans are to be made . . . In Naafi on the other hand . . . the only common factor between one year and the next is that each proves to be as surprising, capricious and unpredictable as any other period in Naafi's history.'

Heading the list of unpredictables were crises abroad. Naafi was still spread over some forty countries and when a flare up occurred anywhere the personnel had to be augmented, supplies laid on and premises found at a moment's notice. In the late 1940s and the 1950s Naafi was involved in war in Korea, civil war in Palestine and Cyprus, terrorism in Malaya and Kenya, troubles in the Canal Zone of Egypt and Borneo, nuclear exercises in the Monte Bello Islands and Christmas Island, and of course continued service in Germany. Europe was and still is Naafi's biggest overseas theatre and, apart from such events as the Berlin airlift, the only one that remains reasonably predictable over a long period.

The blockade of West Berlin, imposed by the Russians in 1948, was broken after several months by an airlift of goods carried by American and British aircraft over the Russian zone to the beleaguered city. From Wunsdorf near Hanover Naafi worked twenty-four hours a day loading aircraft with supplies and providing refreshments for crews and ground staff from a tented canteen on the airfield. A Naafi 'mobile' was the first of a convoy of vehicles to enter Berlin when the blockade was lifted. It was needed urgently because the men at the Berlin end of the airlift had only a single converted lorry to provide them with a day and night service. Naafi had stayed with the British forces in West Berlin, an island surrounded by a hostile power, not exactly besieged but living in conditions of uneasy truce.

Otherwise life has been comfortable for Naafi and its customers in West Germany. For ten years after the end of the war the headquarters were at the pleasant spa Bad Salzuflen ('Bath Salts' to the Naafi staff) and moved when the Forces' headquarters was established at Rheindahlen near München Gladbach. Routine was punctuated by social events: Naafi handled the catering at the Rhine Army Horse Show; and by occasional vigorous action, as at the autumn manoeuvres of NATO (North Atlantic Treaty Organisation) in 1954, when Naafi ran thirty-three mobile canteens for 137,000 British, Dutch, Belgian, Canadian and American troops.

During its first ten years in Germany Naafi's main distributing warehouse had been in Hamburg. In 1954 BAOR decided for military and political reasons to move its supply points west of the Rhine and Naafi transferred the warehouse and transport depot to Waldniel. There it employed 450 German staff, many of whom had been sent to Totteridge for training, and the warehouse supplied 400 Naafi canteens, clubs and shops throughout West Germany. Expecting a long stay, Naafi was allotted a colony of suburban houses, known colloquially as Naafi Alley, for its senior staff. But within three years they had to move the base to an even larger centre at Krefeld, where a Naafi township was created comprising warehouse, transport garage and workshop, power house, staff hostel, staff club, bakery, and the inevitable mineral water factory, all surrounded by an unclimbable security fence. The removal was a massive operation and a triumph of organisation. The man in charge said that a fiver would have covered the losses in transit. A case of whisky which fell off a lorry was found by a German civilian who took it to a lost property office and was rewarded with ten per cent of the value.

Krefeld had the first electronic computer in any Naafi establishment, installed by the plans and methods department to handle warehouse accounting. It produced invoices and maintained running stock figures. Naafi's first self-service grocery shop in Germany was opened at Bielefeld in Westphalia, a couple of months after Fontainebleau, and others followed within weeks. Instalment credit terms were first offered to the Forces in Germany. Within a year 7,000 people had bought goods to the value of £180,000, concentrating in the early weeks on such utilitarian items as washing machines, spin dryers and convector heaters but before long adventuring into such purchases as sets of golf clubs. The first big orders came from the canteen manager in a British warship who supplied goods to the value of £600, including half a dozen gold wrist watches at £30 each. Before the decade was out the troops were able to hire cars through Naafi and a year or two later buy cars on hire purchase terms.

In 1955 Naafi formed a new department, the European Canteen Service, in response to the changed relationship between Germany and the foreign troops on her soil. These were no longer an army of occupation but the advance forces of Western defence, and the German Federal Republic became once more a sovereign state. More onerous changes soon followed. Naafi's European customers had been shopping for many years with BAFSV (British Armed Forces Special Vouchers) and these were now to be replaced with local currencies. In Germany, including Berlin, Naafi had enjoyed a preferential rate of 40 Deutschemarks to the £ for local purchases of equipment and services since the Deutschemark had replaced the Reichsmark in 1948. The concession was now withdrawn, and the pound was suddenly worth only 11.76 Deutschemarks; although in Berlin it continued at the concessional rate for local services and equipment.

Naafi had foreseen the change months before and made economies to meet it but the long term result was nearly a fourfold increase in all costs: rents, gas, electricity, water, laundry, locally purchased equipment, and wages. The prices of goods in shops and canteens had to be increased, twenty thousand lines repriced and new lists and catalogues printed. There was a rush on Naafi shops to buy the limited stocks of goods at the old prices. The former conquerors were now no more than equal partners with Germany in NATO and had to adjust themselves to the new status.

The changes were not only financial. The NATO powers had to work out their legal status in their German partner's territory, and Naafi arranged to be represented in the discussions through its secretary and legal representative, Mr MacGowan.

For a time the only Naafi base comparable in size and importance with Germany was Egypt. At the end of 1945 the Allied Forces in Egypt were responsible for a territory stretching south through Somaliland and East Africa to Madagascar, north to Greece, east to Persia and west to Tripolitania. But within a year Egypt had become impatient with her dependent role, and a movement started which was to end in the complete expulsion of foreign troops from the country. The first phase was the removal of the British garrisons from the Delta to the Canal Zone early in 1947. This involved among other things re-housing more than 700 Service families who had settled in Cairo and Alexandria. The plan was to build and equip communal villages for them, and Naafi, as a Service organisation, was considered better equipped than civilian caterers to undertake the catering and control. It was given instructions that the standard of living should not be lower than that of a good officers' mess, and it estimated costs and proposed charges to be levied against the residents accordingly. The project was not an immediate success; there were conflicts over costs and difficulties of adjustment to the new conditions; but the War Office helped to ease the financial burden and, with the co-operation of house committees elected by the residents, Naafi was able to establish a satisfactory relationship with the community.

For the Naafi controller, Mr W. Whitehouse, and his staff, all this was additional to the job of moving £2½ million worth of stores from fourteen warehouses and closing down 250 establishments in the Delta amid increasing interference from the hostile population. At the same time Naafi had to organise its retirement along with the troops from Iraq and Syria. The latter illustrated one of the common disabilities under which Naafi operated. Forty canteens had been built in Syria but because of the sudden reversal of military plans not one was opened.

In nearby Palestine, Jew and Arab were at each other's throats

Naafi canteen launch coming in to the warehouse at South Queensferry on the Firth of Forth

The Naafi 21 Club, Antwerp, 1945

'Marble Arch.' Service family shopping. Suez Canal, 1951
Children play 'Ring o' Roses' behind barbed wire. Suez Canal, 1951

and Naafi was caught repeatedly in machine gun cross fire as it organised its evacuation of the territory in the wake of the British army. The least of the troubles was a sudden walk out of all native staff. Then senior British staff took off their coats, manned the counters, drove lorries and shifted crates. Lorries were shot up or commandeered by whichever of the warring sides happened to be dominant in the vicinity. A Naafi factory inspector was held prisoner for four days by Jewish terrorists, and allowed to continue his duties and even go to the cinema but always under armed guard. He was no sooner released than he was captured by Arabs and condemned to death. As he stood before the firing squad he argued so convincingly in fluent Arabic that they let him go free and unharmed.

Over a million pounds worth of saleable goods and assets worth another million were then moved out of Palestine. Some of them, set up at Rafah on the Egyptian frontier, were bombed by the Egyptians, and canteen staff were killed. Naafi helped to shepherd women and children out of Palestine. By June 1948, when the British mandate in Palestine expired, Naafi had left the territory. When the state of Israel was formed soon after, the Israeli army organised its own canteen service on the Naafi pattern and employed old Naafi hands from among its own people.

Not only Palestine but the whole of the Middle East was in a ferment and the deteriorating relations between Britain and Egypt reached a crisis with the abrogation of the 1936 treaty between the two countries in 1952. Within a few hours the Naafi shop in Ismailia was burnt and looted by the mob and women shoppers had to be rescued by British troops. Naafi organised mobile canteens to carry food to the beleaguered families. Immediately upon the ending of the treaty four thousand local employees quit their jobs with Naafi, mainly under official duress, because they had always been happy and loyal employees. Under Naafi's Middle East controller Mr W. D. Haysey, who as an RASC/EFI colonel had served with distinction in Italy during the second world war, everyone from the most senior ranks downwards lent a hand with the most menial essential services. The WVS were particularly helpful, looking after the welfare of Service wives and children and delivering a bread round under constant risk of attack. Naafi appealed in the UK for temporary staff. Within a few days 1,000 men and girls had volunteered and 600 were flown to Egypt in Naafi's biggest airlift.

Britain had had 85,000 troops in the Canal Zone. By June 1956 they had all left. A thirty-five-year continuous Naafi-Egypt association had come to an end. But that was not quite the end of Britain's involvement in Egypt. Later in that year a brief and bitter conflict flared up at Suez, when Egypt seized the Canal, Britain and France landed troops to protect their interests, Israel crossed the frontier into the Sinai peninsula, the Soviet Union threatened intervention, and a third world war was narrowly averted. Naafi had assembled an EFI unit of about a hundred reservists, trained and kitted them out at the Totteridge depot, and sent an advance party to Cyprus, which was now Naafi's HQ for the Middle East. The party, consisting of four officers and eighteen men, followed the British troops into Port Said, and organised a bulk issue store and mobile canteen service with a speed which won the commendation of the DA and QMG, Brigadier J. H. S. Lacey. He wrote in his report, 'The unit has worked itself into the ground and produced a Naafi service which, during the planning days in London, we never thought possible.'

Naafi came out of this political and military disaster creditably to the last. As a United Nations force took over, the Royal Navy assisted the British withdrawal and Naafi as always supplied the cheer. Some of its officers, wearing a United Nations armband as a safeguard, distributed turkeys and Christmas pudding to the salvage fleet.

Jordan was another Middle Eastern country to which British troops, and Naafi with them, returned when fresh troubles arose. They had evacuated the country in June 1957, apparently for good, but the assassination of King Feisal of Iraq and his ministers a year later created a dangerous situation and Britain resumed her task of maintaining order. Jordanians who had served with Naafi were eager to return. Only a few hours after the first planeload of British paratroops had landed in Amman, the manager of the Overseas Canteen Service in London received a cable, 'I am ex-manager Naafi canteen Amman ready for re-employment. Await instructions.'

While the British forces were retiring from Suez, the Naafi contingent in Korea was preparing to leave after seven years' service in war and peace. The war had been precipitated in 1950 when a North Korean army crossed the line of the thirty-eighth parallel established by the United Nations to divide the communist north from the non-communist southern half of the country. A mixed United Nations force, including British troops under American command, fought a fluctuating war which swept from the extreme south-eastern corner of the peninsula to the borders of China in the north and ended in an armistice which restored the status quo. Naafi ensured that when the troops landed the rough and ready comforts of 'Joe's Bar' would be there.

Naafi asked for two hundred volunteers, and was swamped with applications, not only from home but as far away as Aden. It is a remarkable fact that while female staff were difficult to get and to keep for service in some safe and peaceful base in England, more than enough volunteered for the danger and discomfort of a Far Eastern battlefield. And what discomfort! Veterans of the second world war admitted that there had been nothing to equal the hardships of Korea.

Outside the main towns the roads were cart tracks linking the villages, unsuitable for heavy traffic, a river of mud in winter and sending up such dust clouds in summer that lorries had to keep their lights on all day to penetrate the yellow fog. The winter cold was intense. There was a run on pipes instead of cigarettes for the comfort of folding one's stiff hands round the bowl. Hot tea froze if the cup was put on the ground and at fifty degrees below freezing point one had to chip lumps of ice from the water tanks and melt it for shaving. There was no piped water and the native sources were too contaminated to be safe, even for washing, without chemical treatment.

There were no buildings in the wilds of Korea that could be taken over for canteens. By watching the Koreans Naafi learnt how to build roadhouses in the native style with the primitive local materials. They cut down trees for timber, caulked walls with mud and thatched the roof with rice straw. Brightly painted and adorned with hanging signs (one was the Ship Inn sign salvaged from the Western Desert) the buildings were the pride of the British army and the envy of the Americans who were glad to use Naafi when their own canteen service was not available. Troops of twenty-one nations patronised the roadhouses and Naafi tried as far as possible to provide their accustomed delicacies.

The roadhouses received supplies by helicopter and served the men in the firing line by lorry. Some of the lorry drivers were intrepid to the point of recklessness. One of them drove blithely into a tank battle and had to be shunted to cover in order to shield him and his precious cargo from the enemy. Much of Naafi's stock came from Japan or from Hong Kong. It included gift items for the men to send home under the Naafi Forces parcel scheme (which operated also in the Malayan jungle). In the smaller towns of that impoverished country the Naafi shop was the only place where a soldier could buy anything worth while. Naafi people had to resist the temptation to give food or clothing to the Koreans; beggars would have descended upon them like locusts. They did indirectly contribute to local housing; many Koreans built themselves a shack out of discarded Naafi crates and beer barrels. And empty beer bottles became part of the local currency.

Following the armistice, Naafi had four years of peace in Korea. But apart from spells of leave in Japan there were few compensations. The camps up country were enclosed in barbed wire, and only in the cities such as Seoul and Pusan, where Naafi ran rest and recreation facilities for the troops, were conditions much more enjoyable than a siege.

In Malaya as in Korea British troops fought a communist enemy, but this time it was guerilla warfare in dense jungle. Naafi had a two-fold job: to supply the household needs of Service men's families in the towns and to open supply posts in jungle camps for patrols hunting the terrorists. In the most remote areas military and other supplies were dropped to the troops from aircraft. Parachutes which failed to open were called 'candles', and the losses were reported as 'Naafi stores'. To be a scapegoat is no doubt just part of the Naafi service!

At the height of the emergency Naafi operated scores of jungle canteens from Johore Bahru in the south to the Thailand frontier. Many were simply huts located off the roads, roofed with palm leaves and easily dismantled to follow the most mobile of all Naafi's customers. Some were decorated with bus stop signs, gay advertisements and feminine underwear hanging from the rafters. The Malayan operation lasted for some years and involved the removal of whole villages and their re-erection elsewhere to deny cover for the bandits, and resulted eventually in the defeat of the insurgents and the pacification of the country.

Naafi saw action in other parts of South-East Asia, in North Borneo where British troops were sent for training, and in Hong Kong and Singapore. Hong Kong was the scene of some ugly rioting in 1956 provoked by agitators from China. The rioters set fire to a Naafi bakery, and the British and Chinese staffs maintained supplies under the disabilities of stoning by the rioting minorities and an official curfew. Singapore also had civil disturbances at about the same time. Again Chinese staff maintained the service, clerks in the district office volunteering to deliver groceries to families and refusing to accept any payment.

By 1957 the focus of Naafi's overseas operations had changed dramatically. Egypt, which in 1954 had claimed forty per cent of the entire OCS budget, was out of the picture, and Korea, which had been a big second, had shrunk to very minor proportions. The biggest centre in those parts was now Cyprus, where Britain was trying to hold a balance between a Turkish minority and highly trained and efficiently led EOKA guerillas fighting for complete Greek supremacy. The British forces were regarded as an enemy and Naafi was fair game for hit and run assault. Men were advised never to turn their backs to the street even when locking the car door, nor to look in a shop window unless accompanied by someone watching the passers-by. One in six of Naafi's 1,500 employees was a Greek Cypriot and the risk of hostile infiltration was always considerable. The climax came when a time bomb concealed in a settee in a Naafi canteen in Nicosia exploded, killing two RAF men and wounding others. The RAF immediately banned all the 4,000 Greek Cypriots employed in their own camps and barracks and in Naafi establishments. Employees reporting for work the next morning found the entrances barred by armed troops.

For Naafi this caused chaos. Forty-six canteens, seventeen shops, three clubs, two leave centres, offices, transport, bakery and warehouse were all at a standstill. Garrison and Naafi wives helped to maintain essential services. Headquarters in Britain issued an SOS for 500 volunteers in the press and on radio and television. The size of the response was astonishing even to officials who had had previous experience of recruitment in emergencies. The staff coming to work at Imperial Court next morning found queues at the doors; two men had been there since five am. Within four days Naafi had 17,000 applicants. The Passport Office and medical officers worked extra hours to speed 300 on their flight to the war zone. The airlift was the most costly single item in a total extra cost to Naafi of £200,000. Naafi also helped by extending its shop facilities for troops and families whose normal haunts had been placed out of bounds.

The staff were in danger even when the Cypriots had been sacked. Two officials at the butchery in Famagusta, having a final look round the cold store before leaving at the end of the working day, were trapped by EOKA terrorists, who padlocked the door, switched off the lights, and left the men wearing open necked shirts and slacks in a temperature of minus ten degrees with no hope of being found until the staff opened up next morning. By the light of a match the prisoners discovered a cleaver, and taking turns to hack at the door, they had made a hole eighteen inches square in an hour and a half and shouted for help. 'Had that cleaver not been there,' said one of them, 'the stocks of frozen meat would have been increased overnight.'

It was not only in countries with large concentrations of troops and major military operations that Naafi found risk and excitement. There was trouble in Kenya where Naafi served the troops quelling the Mau Mau rebellions. It was a highly mobile operation for canteen staff as well as soldiers. Tented shops and canteens had to be set up suddenly and just as suddenly dismantled and loaded on lorries for transport a couple of hundred miles up country, with the chance of getting bogged down in some remote marsh till rescued by the Royal Engineers. Bahrein was another hot spot where political riots caused a sudden influx of troops and pressure on the small Naafi contingent. In an atmosphere of ninety degrees heat and sixty to eighty degrees humidity and a wind laden with moisture and sand, any movement outside the air conditioned comfort of Naafi's canteens and stores was a torment.

Sometimes Naafi was involved in war while serving British Forces on a peaceful mission. One of the most dramatic was the *Amethyst* incident in 1949 during the Chinese civil war. Sailing up the Yangtse-Kiang to relieve HMS *Consort* as guard ship at the British Embassy at Nanking, HMS *Amethyst* suffered severe casualties (including the CO and the ship's doctor) under heavy fire from the Communists, who frustrated attempts by other British ships to come to her rescue. Transferring her wounded to sampans sent alongside by the Nationalists under cover of night, *Amethyst* sought a safe anchorage and was marooned there for three months. Her eventual escape down the river without further damage or casualties made the headlines in the world's newspapers. Her 22-year-old canteen manager, Mr John McNamara, won high commendation for his services in tending the wounded and helping to plot the ship's progress along the tortuous and dangerous channel. He had an honoured place in the march through Plymouth, and shared in the civic reception for *Amethyst*'s indomitable men.

There were less harassing divergences from the normal Naafi routine. They included a goodwill visit to Leningrad by the Navy and a party organised on board for 500 Russian children. One of Naafi's commissions was to supply 3,600 canteen packs to troops re-enacting Dunkirk for a film, and another to deliver stores to the USS *Nautilus*, the world's first atomic powered submarine, which had entered a British port after its epic 8,000 miles voyage from Honolulu over (perhaps one should say under) the North Pole. The Naafi canteen in an armed net layer on a 40,000 mile cruise in the Antarctic helped to rescue an exploration ship caught in the ice, and replenished its supplies of the only two commodities it was short of – beer and dubbin.

Then there were military and naval exercises. One of these was a beach and port landing at Zeebrugge and a three weeks simulated consolidation of a bridgehead. It enabled Naafi to put its RASC/EFI reservists through their paces. They were drawn from behind the counters at the grocery chains – International Stores, Home and Colonial, Maypole Dairy – and flown into very realistic action, setting up canteen facilities for three camps plus mobiles, a beer bar and a grocery shop. Naafi staff participated in a very different operation in 1954 aboard the aircraft carrier HMS *Warrior*, which made two trips to bring a total of 3,000 Vietnamese refugees from Haiphong to Saigon. Extra blankets, camp beds and rice had to be taken aboard and medical attention laid on for the old and sick: several infants were born en route. The flight deck, festooned with loaded clothes lines, took on the appearance of an Indo-Chinese street. As the ship reached port the officers' mess, the ship's fund and the canteen manager subscribed towards a supply of cigarettes, sweets and chocolates to console the exiles.

So necessary had Naafi become to the armed forces that no expedition was undertaken by any unit without its ministrations. For a few months in 1953 Naafi had the rare experience of setting up shop on a desert island in support of a mixed Services and scientific team which was to test Britain's first atomic weapon. Landing on one of the otherwise uninhabited Monte Bello islands off the coast of Western Australia, a sixteen strong Naafi party netted off a small bay to make a shark-free swimming pool and opened a canteen alongside. Other canteens followed; one of them, worthy of Robinson Crusoe, was made of converted packing cases and labelled Ruxley Towers. While the scientists prepared the launching site and then waited for the wind to change so that the product of the explosion would be carried in a safe direction, the crews of the escorting fleet enjoyed leisure activities for which wealthy tourists pay high prices in tropical playgrounds – shark fishing (the Naafi shop in the flagship did a roaring trade in three-inch shark hooks), turtle stabbing, swimming in sun-warmed waters, and less exotic pursuits such as boxing, football and cinema shows.

The explosion four years later of a hydrogen bomb on Christmas Island in the Gilbert group was a larger exercise in every way. The island had a native population swollen by 5,000 Service men, fifty Naafi personnel who lived in Army quarters, and two WVS housed in huts built on stilts to exclude the swarms of land crabs which were almost the only wild life in that barren land. Naafi established two canteens, a gift shop, beer bar, bulk issue stores and a mineral water factory. A supply ship called once in six months, but Naafi had an allowance to spend in Honolulu on goods which came daily by air along with the mail. Two small hospitals were built on the island, one for the Army and the RAF and the other for the Navy.

Apart from leave spent in Honolulu and the eventual explosion of the bomb, life was monotonous for the men. They had a swimming pool, and the WVS worked seven days a week to provide entertainments, tombolas and a library service. Otherwise leisure was focused on the bar, which could take as much as £100 in three hours on a busy night. The Naafi shop was popular: the men could buy gifts to send home or have flowers delivered to their womenfolk, though the flowers were certainly not grown on the barren coral dust which Christmas Island had instead of soil. The troops were paid in sterling, which circulated within a very narrow orbit. It was spent with Naafi, who banked it with the paymaster, who paid the men, who spent their money with Naafi, and so on indefinitely. Christmas Island presented a microcosm of a national economy.

When the time came to detonate the hydrogen bomb, the Gilbertese and the WVS were taken off the island, the native booby birds and the canteen cat were shut away in safety, and the Naafi staff were directed to the shelter of a palm grove where they stood with hands over their closed eyes and backs to the scene of action while a voice counted out the seconds till the blinding flash was over and it was safe to look round at the mushroom cloud. The purpose of nearly a year's absence from home was completed in a few seconds.

Naafi was much involved with islands in the 1950s. The last of them was Gan, a speck in the Indian Ocean 600 miles south-west of Ceylon, smaller than Heathrow Airport and leased from the ruler of the Maldive Islands to serve as an RAF staging post. For this purpose the island had to be completely cleared: the inhabitants re-housed in neighbouring islands, their village obliterated, and a runway built across the middle of the island to make it in effect a static aircraft carrier for the defence of Commonwealth communications to India and the Far East. The British Forces were no strangers to the islanders: the atoll of which Gan formed a part had provided anchorage in its lagoon for ships of the Royal Navy since the early years of the second world war. Now the Maldivians were eager to come over in their boats from other islands in the archipelago to work alongside the British and Pakistanis building the base. One of them earned extra pay as a 'knocker up', calling early in the morning to waken the resident workers. When their day's work was finished the Maldivians would be checked out by the RAF police, then wade to their boats to take home to their various atolls purchases from the Naafi store, the larger objects carried on their heads and the smaller ones loaded into umbrellas held upside down and bought from Naafi merely to be used as containers.

Before the British Forces took charge the Gan islanders, making a poor subsistence out of fishing, were undernourished and hardly fit for manual work. With good pay, spent in the Naafi shop, their diet and health improved enormously. On one occasion Naafi had surplus tins of syrup and of herrings, and presented them to its Maldivian friends, but omitted to explain how these unfamiliar foodstuffs should be consumed. The Maldivians invented their own recipe. They scooped the centre out of a loaf of bread, poured in herrings and syrup, and ate the mixture with relish. It has since become a national dish.

Almost everything had to be imported, even vegetables, which some of the canteen staff tried in vain to grow on the island. Naafi was the universal provider, serving the Forces, the contractors' men and the local people. It handled all the messing, provided canteens (a separate one serving Pakistani dishes), hairdresser, cobbler and tailor, running a bakery and a mineral water factory, and also supplying consumer goods to the Maldivian Co-operative Society. Among the goods bought by the Society were powdered camphor for embalming, kerosene, refrigerators, bicycles, sarongs, furniture, crockery, watches, and mill puff for stuffing cushions. The Pakistanis bought radios to take home, and the Service customers bought every kind of product from bars of chocolate to tape recorders.

The variety and modernity of the goods available on this remote island showed how far Naafi had advanced in a decade. Troops operating in primitive locations had no longer to be content with a primitive service. They could afford fairly expensive ways of relieving the tedium, and Naafi, with the aid of air and sea transport, was able to supply the means. Though Naafi's total business worldwide had diminished, customers were spending much more. Average expenditure per head in the UK was twenty-four shillings a week compared with fourteen shillings in 1950. There had been other changes; fewer clubs and canteens (522 against 736); fewer counter service shops (207 against 370); but among the innovations since 1950 were 137 'walk-in' shops for members of the Forces, 118 self-service shops for their families, and 1,331 slot machines.

This changing character needed a new symbol to represent it.

As Naafi approached its fortieth birthday the board of management decided to drop for most purposes the old-fashioned crest that had served since the foundation and replace it with something that proclaimed an up to date commercial organisation. The new design was a letter N composed of three links to represent the three participating Services. It was starkly simple and suitable for use on stationery, literature, containers and vehicles to create a powerful corporate image. Significantly, it focused public attention upon N for Naafi, and relegated the official title, The Navy, Army and Air Force Institutes, to the dusty places where formalities were still required.

CHAPTER FIVE

Progress in the Sixties

As Naafi entered upon its fifth decade it was subjected to the most searching official scrutiny since its formation. The Service departments wanted to be sure that Naafi was structurally sound; that the customer was getting value for money and not being exploited; that Naafi, as constituted, would continue to be necessary to the armed forces in the absence of a major war. Naafi's services were known to be unequal, excellent at their best but sometimes falling short of needs. The Services wanted to know who or what was at fault and how the defects could be remedied.

Naafi had not neglected to look at itself with a critical eye. It had appointed the Howitt committee in 1954 (referred to in the preceding chapter), and had made changes in its organisation and methods in the UK as a result of the committee's recommendation. But the Services were not satisfied. Their misgivings were caused partly by vague murmurings from the field, and partly by imperfect knowledge of what Naafi could and could not be expected to do; but the existence of misunderstanding was a defect in itself and justification for an inquiry from outside Naafi's ranks. One such inquiry in 1957 was started by the Quarter-Master-General, who invited Army Commanders-in-Chief at home and overseas to give their candid opinion of Naafi and suggest where it could be improved. Their comments were, on the whole, very favourable. They realised that shortcomings in the standard of service of Naafi's staff were due to the peculiar demands of the Services in regard to location of premises and hours of work, and they admitted the inadequacy of accommodation in the older barracks. Naafi, they agreed, was trying to eliminate faults for which it was responsible, but they thought its publicity and public relations could be improved. They asked for more self-service in the shops (this was already being provided by Naafi). They approved of Naafi's performance and price policy in Germany, and for the most part elsewhere, but thought that troops in isolated stations should be compensated for any necessarily high prices through local overseas allowances. They recommended that Naafi should share more of the privileges and conditions of army personnel.

A very different verdict came from a committee appointed by the Army Council in June 1958, composed of Army and civilian members under the chairmanship of General Sir Lashmer Whistler. It was formed to report on discipline, training schools, quarters, and other matters concerning the new All-Regular Army, and contained a section on Naafi. Unlike the QMG's inquiry, it reported widespread dissatisfaction with Naafi, found Naafi too large, impersonal and unenterprising, its prices too high, its shop service poor, its expensive town clubs contrasting with dreary little canteens in unit barracks, though the report admitted that here the Army was to blame. The committee suggested alternatives to Naafi: either let the Army run its own canteen service; or abolish the rebate and contribution to Service charities and finance the canteens from Army funds; or open the canteen service to competition from contractors. The committee, aware of the superficial character of their research on Naafi, recommended an inquiry under an independent chairman.

It was probably the Whistler report that prompted the big and very thorough investigation into Naafi's structure and operations which reported in 1961. A committee, with a distinguished membership drawn from business and the Services under the chairmanship of Mr John Corbett, was appointed by the Service departments 'to review the status and operations of Naafi in the light of the needs of the future All-Regular Forces, both in normal and operational conditions, and to make recommendations'. The members visited establishments in the UK and overseas, and took evidence from Service departments, Naafi, the WVS and other voluntary welfare organisations.

On the whole, Naafi came very well out of the examination. The committee declared that Naafi was basically sound and the need for it beyond question. It was to continue to operate wherever the armed forces were deployed, without regard to the profitability of any particular establishment; but, as a source of funds for Service welfare, it had to remain economically viable. That, of course, was and still is the eternal dilemma of Naafi, as the committee well realised, but 'We stress the need to be "profit conscious",' they said, 'because our observation has convinced us that it is not appreciated at all levels in the organisation, nor indeed in the Services.' They acknowledged that Naafi had tried to meet the demands of an increasingly affluent clientele, and urged it to provide facilities for greater diversity of trading. In order to achieve this, Naafi must plough back funds for development and improvement. It should be bolder in the employment of its financial resources, either by acquiring premises which the State was not obliged to provide but which it would pay Naafi to have, or in cases where the State was responsible but public funds were not immediately available, by advancing the money and awaiting reimbursement. 'Generally speaking, Naafi has waited for the State to provide facilities, and it has frequently missed commercial opportunities which might have been taken if it had made use of its own resources.'

That was true enough, but there was good reason. Naafi had used its own funds (it still does) to modernise and improve facilities which were the responsibility of the State; but reimbursement has often been delayed excessively, with consequent strain on Naafi's resources. Similar reservations apply to another of the committee's comments: while giving Naafi credit for improvements in canteens and shops, they said that some establishments were unnecessarily shabby and too institutional in appearance. Here, again, Naafi had to make the best of premises which, especially in barracks, were not its property or of its choosing.

A Corbett recommendation which, to Naafi's regret, was not accepted was that the Services should provide free fuel, heat and light in unit canteens. Naafi pointed out that during part of the day at least it provided what was in effect the Forces' industrial canteen, and it was customary for industrial canteens to be subsidised. The Services accepted the recommendation that Naafi should tender for catering contracts in competition with civilian caterers, but the report emphasised the need for ensuring that Naafi should be enabled to retain a fair share of this business. Naafi had to remind the Service departments that if it were to be squeezed out of this field it would be in no position to provide a service if a canteen contractor should drop out.

The Corbett committee pointed out that it was uneconomical to provide separate accommodation for corporals in clubs and canteens. This is a problem of which Naafi has always been well aware, and it will be considered at greater length in another chapter. Naafi is closer to the customer and therefore more sensitive to undercurrents of feeling than committees of inquiry can be. When junior ranks say, 'We see enough of the so-and-sos most of the time; we can do without them off duty,' Naafi has to be cautious about mixing the breeds. The town clubs, started soon after the second world war, had been an experiment, not entirely successful, in mixing ranks, units and Services. The committee had something to say about these clubs, recommending that the need for each should be re-examined (this was in fact already being done), and gave its blessing to the new 'social club' concept, which, as will be seen, was to supersede the town clubs.

Much of what appeared in the report was a restatement of what already existed or was being undertaken by Naafi. Its value, however, lay in its endorsement of Naafi's broad structure and policies. The committee recommended enlarging the board of management to include a chairman and a deputy chairman, four or five other part time directors, three full time executive directors (one of them the managing director) and, as before, one full time member from each of the three Services. They advised that the Service members of the board should be chosen for their known aptitude for and interest in such work and for experience in administration, rather than their exclusively operational work. The committee found that the Service members had no clear terms of reference or instruction on their responsibilities, or on how to keep in touch with the needs of Service people, and recommended that the Service departments should seek ways of making them responsible for passing on to the Naafi headquarters matters raised by customers at meetings of Institute committees, wives' committees, and anywhere else.

The Corbett committee's major contribution, however, was to point out a structural weakness which had persisted much too long: that was, the inadequacy of the Naafi council as then constituted. 'The council's prestige,' says Mr Prideaux, the present chairman of Naafi, 'was the reverse of what has been traditionally said of the harlot: she had power without responsibility, they had responsibility without power.' The power rested with the Service ministries, and their representatives on the Naafi council were figureheads. The board reported to the council and presented its accounts every six months in what was not much more than a shareholders' meeting, at which the council received 'such glimpses of future plans as the board of management revealed'. On major policy issues the board dealt direct with the Service ministries.

The committee recommended that both power and responsibility should be combined in a newly formed council composed of the people to whom the board reported effectively in Whitehall. Such a council would have sufficient standing to give and obtain rapid decisions. The committee advocated a reduction in the size of the council from twelve to six members, with the option of co-opting additional members. They should meet quarterly or more often.

The changes on the council were made almost immediately. The principal administrative officer of each Service department – the Fourth Sea Lord, the Quarter-Master-General and the Air Member for Supply and Organisation – became members, together with the Deputy Under-Secretary (General Policy and Finance) Admiralty, the Deputy Under-Secretary of State War Office, and the Director-General of Personal Services Air Ministry. The seventh member was the chairman of the board of management, who thus stood astride of both bodies.

The president of the council is chosen from among the members and each Service is represented in turn. The PAOs hold their position for three years. Under the memorandum of association, membership of the council is a personal matter and cannot be delegated. This means that the chairman of the board is personally in touch with the people who matter at the seat of power and that the Ministry of Defence maintains continuity of association with Naafi.

Sir William Beale had planned to retire from Naafi in February 1960, but agreed to stay until the Corbett committee had reported. He had presided over a large scale modernisation, particularly in the shops, which had been brought into line with the latest trends in retail trade. But profound changes in kind, as well as in scale and quality of service, had begun to take place. When an Army sergeant stationed in Germany could call at a Naafi shop, order an £800 car and pay on the nail in cash, it was time to realise that Naafi was no longer simply the grocer and provision merchant of the armed forces. Sir William Beale believed that Naafi now required a chairman with something more than grocery experience. That wider retail experience entered with his successor Mr (now Sir) Rex Cohen.

Mr Cohen, former Lieutenant-Colonel and an Assistant Quarter-Master-General Second Army, was a department store man, familiar not only with food and grocery but with the whole range of consumer durables as chairman of Lewis's Investment Trust, which had recently acquired Selfridges. He brought with him from Lewis's one of the group's senior executives, Mr B. A. Stapleton, as a joint general manager to help in formulating merchandising policy. Mr Cohen attended the first meeting of the newly constituted council and made Naafi history as the first chairman of the board of management to occupy a seat on the council. Like his predecessors he went on tour soon after his appointment to see Naafi at work at home, in Europe and the Far East.

Other big administrative changes took place at about the same time. Sir Randle Feilden, after eleven years with the Corporation, retired from the post of managing director but remained on the board. Mr Humphrey Prideaux, who had held the position of managing director jointly with Sir Randle for a year, now became sole managing director. In 1964 he succeeded Sir Rex Cohen as chairman. Though not a Naafi product – he had had twenty years in the Army before joining the Corporation as personnel manager in 1953 – he was the first chairman to be appointed from within the organisation.

Unlike previous chairmen who were substantial businessmen before joining the Naafi board, Mr Prideaux became associated with other businesses while a member of Naafi. He has thus been able not only to bring experience gained on the boards of Brooke Bond Liebig, W. H. Smith and Son, Metropolitan Life Assurance and London Life Assurance to bear upon Naafi, but also to compare Naafi's practice and progress with those old-established and prosperous commercial enterprises from a fresh angle. Having graduated to the chair through the personnel department, Mr Prideaux has excelled on the human side of management. His long career in the Army taught him what the Forces wanted. He has raised the quality of Naafi people by selection and training and improved working conditions and rewards. In those and other ways he helped to boost the reputation of Naafi.

For three years Mr Prideaux was both chairman and managing director. This looked like a retrograde step, but it was necessary in order to develop a strong top executive management out of the organisation's own manpower resources. On 1st January 1968 Mr Edward MacGowan, who had become assistant managing director in 1966, took over as chief executive. The chairman retained some executive responsibility till the end of the decade. The chairmanship then reverted to its former function, as a part time honorary office completely non-executive and concerned solely with policy.

The management faced a new challenge in the 1960s. The post-war rundown of the service, its consolidation within the smaller dimension and adjustment to changing social conditions had been completed, and generally endorsed by the defence departments through the Corbett enquiry. Now Naafi had to aim at growth, in spite of conditions which made for further shrinkage. While the British armed forces withdrew from one country after another and Naafi sales continued to be restricted to this diminishing market, the management had to seek increased turnover and profit by selling

Naafi Roadhouse in Korea, 1953. Helicopter landing site on right of picture

Coronation catering, 2nd June 1953

A British soldier guards Service wives at Naafi shop, Larnaca, Cyprus, 1958

more to the few, and reduce costs by administrative skill and operational efficiency. Some of the improvements arose out of the four-year 'Kent' experiment in stock control. Naafi chose a well defined self-contained area of the Home Service in Kent in which a small warehouse supplied thirty establishments, collected data on consumer demand and sales flow of commodities, and introduced a pilot scheme of automatic stock control for 600 items based on the computer at the London headquarters. Some of the controlled lines were found to be in poor demand, and it soon proved possible to reduce the 600 items to 450 and eventually to 280. The experiment was then extended to all the lines held at the warehouse and similar reductions were achieved.

The next step was to code the goods, reorganise the layout of the shops in line with the coding, and provide the managers with a system of ordering which would avoid overstocking, indicate which were the fast and which the slow sellers, and enable the central merchandising department to short-list the items which every shop was required to stock. The Kent findings were extended into Naafi shops throughout the country. Clutter was cleaned up and presentation modernised. Back room space was saved, capital released, stockturn accelerated and no sales lost by throwing out dead lines.

Computers have played a vital part in the rationalisation of Naafi's business processes. Naafi was among the early users of electronic aids in retailing and catering, reorganising its clerical work so that more of it could be put on to the computer, and replacing its original equipment with more up to date models as successive generations of computers emerged to extend the possibilities of office automation. As with most of Naafi's innovations, electronic data processing was first applied in Germany. In 1956 two Stantec Zebra computers were installed in the Krefeld warehouse, and were replaced in August 1966 by a Honeywell 200. This machine is today the heart of a stock control and accounting system covering about 10,000 lines held in the warehouse. The first Naafi computer in the UK was a Honeywell 400 installed in December 1963, replaced in June 1967 by a Honeywell 1200, and joined by a second H 1200 in April 1970 to double the computer capacity at Kennington.

One of the more obvious functions of a computer is to process the payroll. At Kennington the computers calculate wages and salaries for 9,000 weekly paid UK staff and 2,000 monthly paid officials, taking into account tax deductions, bonus and overtime additions, and other variations of the standard rates. At the same time the computer produces employee statistics required by the

H

management. The ordinarily austere routine occasionally has its lighter side. On one occasion, by an error in programming (computers are said to be infallible and only man can err) a female member of the staff was recorded in the computer as a male. In pre-computer days one made the correction with a pen or tore up a piece of paper, but computers cannot be corrected so easily. The denatured lady had to be sacked, reappointed immediately in her own character, and the fact fed into the computer. In compensation for its occasional eccentricities, the computer performs calculations at the rate of several million per second, which no human being will ever emulate.

While the London office was being increasingly computerised, Naafi's accounts centre in Nottingham began to receive similar treatment. The Honeywell 200 installed there in January 1967 was upgraded in little over a year to H 1200. Employed wholly on accounts, the Nottingham instrument illustrates strikingly the reduction in paper work achieved by replacing manual with automatic procedures. In the pre-computer era, enormous packages of documents used to pass between Nottingham and London. Now the same quantity of data comes on a small roll of magnetic tape.

Behind the dry facts of successive computer replacements and upgradings there is a triumph of integration which puts Naafi in line with the most modern businesses. The establishment of compatible computers in the three centres – London, Nottingham and Krefeld – provides an integrated management information system which is essential for an organisation engaged in such a variety of activities spread so widely over the world. Instead of having separate data storage in each area and slow and cumbersome communication among them, all are now linked in an automatic circuit of information, applicable to each activity and providing for the needs of the organisation as a whole. One result has been a simplified ordering system, enabling managers of shops and clubs in the UK to replenish stocks by sending their requirements in coded form to a central point. These are fed into the computer, which determines the source of supply for each item and produces the necessary orders and invoices.

Naafi's marketing in London and Germany has benefited from the computer facilities. The marketing department can learn quickly and continuously the volume of each line taken up by each establishment and to what extent sales follow. So the department can ensure without delay that goods which sell well in some establishments are stocked in others. They can check up on the success of new lines and eliminate in good time those which have ceased to be popular.

The marketing function was formed into a separate department in 1968 to interpret and apply the computer findings and conduct research in the field. Market research has influenced the design of shops and the facilities offered. Naafi's modern supermarkets differ from their counterparts in the general run of retailing in the range of goods and services available. They are more like miniature department stores. The Service wife can not only buy groceries and wines but also pots and pans, children's clothes, a refrigerator, electric fire or vacuum cleaner. She can have the more expensive items on credit terms. Instalment credit sales were an immediate success from the customer's point of view but, for a time, a mixed blessing to Naafi owing to an accumulation of slow payers. Unlike hire purchase, the goods on credit become the property of the purchaser after the first down payment following the deposit and cannot be recovered, in the last resort, except by legal action – a rare event fortunately. The mobility of the Forces causes complications. The family follows where the soldier is drafted, and a credit transaction started in Aldershot may have to be completed in Hong Kong. In the long run the individual shop's gains and losses are evened out, but in the short term the manager has worries which his fellows in the retail chains never know.

The biggest Naafi supermarket in the UK is at Tidworth in Wiltshire and the most eccentric – architecturally that is – at Aldershot. The diamond-shaped Aldershot building, with a roof that is all curves, crests and slopes like a mountain landscape with ski runs, created quite a stir in design circles, but would perhaps have been more suitable for a concert hall than for a complex of goods on display, cash desks and offices. One of the roof ridges, coming down almost to pavement level, was a godsend to the little boys of Aldershot who used it as a slide and doubled the parental bill for shorts. It has since been made boyproof by a small structural alteration.

Naafi's first shopping arcade in the UK was opened at the RAF station at Marham, Norfolk, in 1966. It brought to a Service community of 800 families, on a station remote from big town shopping, the facilities of a miniature High Street. Set back from a roofed terrace were a food hall, butcher's shop, patisserie and greengrocer, ladies', children's and men's wear departments, a gifts and household shop, a branch of Lloyds bank, dry cleaning, shoe repairs and hairdressing; and behind the arcade are a car park and a Naafi-operated petrol station.

Competitors for the Service wife's money in Naafi's environment are well armed, and Naafi has introduced some powerful incentives to beat the field. The latest is a bonus dividend. The customer receives dividend stamps (a shilling stamp for every one pound spent) and, when she has collected four pounds worth, can exchange them for a bonus certificate worth five pounds to be spent in any Naafi shop or on goods in a Naafi catalogue. Since these purchases are eligible for ordinary Naafi discount the customer enjoys multiple gains.

None of these incentives would be effective if prices were not competitive in themselves. In the Home Service, Naafi carries out continuous price testing throughout the year and, in addition, three times a year an independent agency makes tests. Prices in Naafi shops are shown to be often below the average of the test sample before any allowance is made for discount or dividend.

A special kind of shop has been developed during the 1960s for the convenience of the Service man (and in many places his wife, too) who does not want to queue at the supermarket for a simple purchase of cigarettes, a few handkerchiefs or a roll of film. Called originally 'walk-in' shops but now Services shops, they are usually built as annexes to the clubs, and their stock is generally limited to the smaller articles and more casual purchases.

Vending machines are a further aid to quick sales, and there are now so many of them that it has paid Naafi to have its own maintenance staff. Experiments have been made in enlarging the range of vending machine sales. Beer was tried out, appropriately, at the Hampshire village of Middle Wallop. (It is not true that they have a weaker brew at neighbouring Nether Wallop, or a more potent one at Over Wallop.) Vending machines are vulnerable to an obvious form of exploitation. When emptied by the staff they yield coins of more than a dozen countries in addition to our own. At least Naafi cannot complain of a shortage of foreign currency! The takings have also included a quantity of discs and tokens that are nobody's legal tender, and even on one occasion three indigestion tablets. The delinquents are hoist with their own trickery when they get the jackpot from a 'one-armed bandit' in the club and take away a quantity of unspendable metal.

The slot machines fulfil a double purpose, to relieve the problem of finding staff and to provide an ever-open service of snacks. These machines started as accessories to pubs, shops and restaurants, but developed into automatic cafeteria, consisting of banks of vending units selling a popular range of eatable, drinkable and smokeable goods. There is of course – so far – a limit to the substitution of human service by machines; the Naafi girl still presides at tavern and bar lounges in the clubs.

Naafi clubs have been transformed in the sixties. The town clubs have been closed one after another and the buildings sold. The loss they had been making was not their most serious defect: Naafi is reconciled to losing money in providing a necessary service. But when patronage shrank till the rooms were almost empty it was obvious that the town clubs had outlived their need. In the years immediately following the war, especially during National Service, they provided amenities which the troops could not readily find outside, but as the social opportunities in the garrison towns multiplied the Service man became much less dependent on these clubs for his amusements. He still needed places in barracks and stations where he could find quiet, comfort and refreshment, but some re-thinking was needed. The outcome was a new concept, the social club, not fundamentally different from the town clubs, embodying many of their valuable qualities and profiting by the high standard they had set, but differing in orientation to suit the changing outlook and circumstances of Service people.

It was the Navy that suggested and started the new type of club. The prototype was the Heron Club at the Royal Naval Air Service station, Yeovilton, in Somerset, nicknamed the Wrendezvous because women of the Naval Service used it as well as the men. The sailors and WRNS set a pattern also in organisation. They formed a committee to administer the rules and had the right to ban a persistent offender. The RAF soon followed the Navy's lead in giving practical expression to the club concept, but the Army was hesitant. Naafi proposed, with the collaboration of the Army authorities, to convert at its own expense one Junior Ranks Club in each of the twelve Naafi regions in the UK. The result was convincing up to a point, and the Army eventually adopted the new concept as an improvement upon the old JRC pattern. But the new clubs have fitted less smoothly into Army life than into that of the other Services, because of circumstances peculiar to the Army, which will be discussed in the next chapter along with some speculation on the future of Naafi

Every year throughout the 1960s, at home and overseas, clubs were being built on the new principle and existing ones renovated in the new style. The modern clubs at Aldershot, the home of the British Army, are typical, offering tavern bars fitted with the latest automatic glass-washing machines and infra-red equipment for hot snacks; lounges carpeted and furnished in excellent taste; games and billiard rooms, television, hairdressing saloon (an outside concession) and, in one case, an untypical wives' room where the ladies can hold social gatherings or fashion displays while their menfolk are on manoeuvres. The soldiers can entertain wives or girl friends in a gracious environment; the WRAC can invite a man friend to a drink or a dance at their own tastefully designed club.

A two-way influence is discernible in the new clubs. They reflect the more cultivated tastes of the young men recruited to the Forces but they have also helped to improve the behaviour of the more careless elements. When the canteen furniture and fittings were rough, they were treated roughly, but the good furniture and furnishings of the new clubs, scrupulously maintained, are treated with more respect. It is rare indeed for anyone to scribble on the polished woodwork or stub out his cigarette on the quite expensive fabrics. From Naafi's point of view the outlay in quality has proved an economy.

The clubmen are actively involved through their committees in making their membership worth while. They organise many of their own amusements and some invite quite well known entertainers to put on a show. Naafi is also paying more specific attention to the clubs as a result of recent changes in the pattern of district management. In the past the district managers were responsible for all shops as well as clubs within a geographical area. Now, wherever geography permits, they are being reorganised on a functional rather than a geographical basis, so that a district manager will supervise only one kind of establishment – shops or clubs – within a larger area. Another change has been made to promote some of the women restaurant and welfare superintendents to district managers and so open up more rewarding careers for women employees.

Among the newer additions to the services for the Forces and their families are bowling alleys and petrol filling stations. Through Naafi the Service man can now buy life insurance and thus have the same opportunity as civilians to provide for the future. Naafi's supplies department has ranged ever more widely to find goods in variety at reasonable prices for its worldwide customers, buying from as many as ten thousand suppliers in all parts of the world. The number of lines carrying the Naafi trademark is growing continually and includes many best sellers. Naafi's own brand of instant coffee now accounts for 81 per cent of all its coffee sales in the UK, biscuits 85 per cent, jam 81 per cent and washing up liquid 80 per cent. Naafi is now a big wine merchant, handling 1,300 lines of wines and spirits and bottling 150 different wines. It stores some 25,000 dozen bottles in cellars on Kennings Way which also house the bottling plant.

Though Naafi is doing more of its own manufacturing and processing it can never be self-contained, except perhaps in one kind of product, and that is printing. Its printing works, known as The Forces Press, removed in 1961 from London to Aldershot, can cope with all Naafi's printing requirements and much of those of the three Services. It prints *Naafi News* (the staff journal), the Corporation's annual report, all Naafi's booklets and forms, the massive loose leaf instruction book issued to every shop and club manager, the manual of recipes and prices, and sales and publicity material of all kinds – and indeed anything of a non-routine character such as this Jubilee history. For the three Services the press produces half a million Christmas cards a year die stamped with individual crests, regimental magazines and sports programmes, invitation cards, camp guides and posters, visiting cards and stationery. Its letterpress, offset and die stamping machines also handle work in monochrome and colour for other printers.

Valuable additional business comes to Naafi from supplying messes. The mess wine trade, in particular, grew enormously during the 1960s. Of about 540 messes in the UK the great majority buy most (and in some cases all) of their wines and spirits and other bar supplies from Naafi, and the proportion of mess customers is much higher overseas. Many messes run cellar accounts with Naafi and have the advantage of paying on consumption. Naafi keeps and enlarges this trade against powerful competition by cutting profits almost to vanishing point

A special assignment of unusual interest, starting in 1962, was to cater for 1,700 Gurkhas stationed at Tidworth and accompanied by 480 wives and children. Naafi did some preliminary research into their diet and religious customs so that – weather always excepted – the strangers should feel at home. Their native foods, including vitaminised rice, fresh coconut, limes and 'ghi' (cooking fat) were imported, and sold in a special family shop along with betel nut (the Gurkhas' equivalent of chewing gum), a large selection of spices, several kinds of joss stick and incense for use at worship, and red powders for making caste and marriage marks on the forehead. These tough little warriors from the mountains of Nepal needed no interpreters; many had come from families with a long record of service in the British Army.

Among the more orthodox catering efforts were luncheon and dinner parties for the Jubilee of the Women's Services, the Corps of Commissionaires, the commemoration of Waterloo (attended by the

Queen, Prince Philip, the present Duke of Wellington and other descendants of the Iron Duke), and Founders Day at the Royal Chelsea Hospital; and spectacular events such as the Battle of Britain display at Biggin Hill, the Aldershot Horse Show, the World Gliding Championships entered by thirty nations, the display of fighting vehicles, and the Falcon sky diving display, when two members of the team made a delayed parachute dive from six thousand feet, holding the Naafi flag between them. Naafi sent a mobile canteen to Copenhagen to look after the needs of 750 officers and men taking part in the Military Tattoo in British Week. It remained open from 6 am to midnight and had a continual stream of customers for duty-free cigarettes and tea and snacks, at Naafi, not Danish, prices. At a review of the Nato fleet by the Queen at Spithead, Naafi was asked by nine of the twelve nations represented to supply their ships. As part of the service, Naafi laid on two fast vessels for the ice cream run to the American ships.

An overseas commission which has never been officially under Naafi's name, though it has always drawn eighty per cent of its supplies from Krefeld, comes from Allied Forces Central Europe (AFCENT). At its headquarters at Brunssum in Holland, AFCENT has 2,500 Services personnel (three-quarters of them in equal proportions American, British and German and the rest from Canada, Holland, Belgium and Luxembourg) and 1,700 families. Naafi provides the technical know-how and supervisory staff but operates under the AFCENT canteen board.

The Royal Household continued to call upon Naafi for catering services to the palace staffs, and of course the Royal Yacht *Britannia* had its canteen like the ships of the Royal Navy. For the investiture of the Prince of Wales, Naafi organised a Services shop and a tented bar, and provided among other refreshments, 7,000 packaged pies for troops and police.

Naafi was often asked to provide services for manoeuvres at home and overseas. One of the most unusual orders was for fifty live rabbits and fifty live chickens to supplement the rations of fifty members of the Forces on a survival course in Germany. Evidently nowadays troops are not expected to catch their own game or rob the hen roosts. Some of the overseas assignments for troops on manoeuvre were handled by Naafi's 'Ever-Readies'. These were officially known as RAOC/EFI (formerly RASC), a highly trained corps of reservists available at twelve hours notice to fly anywhere in the world. Two exercises in 1966 took them to locations at the two extremes of temperature; one in the Libyan desert, and the other within the Arctic Circle in Norway where they organised a bulk issue storefortroopsengaged onaNATOsurvival course. The Ever-Readies took their turn at military duties and gained useful knowledge of the goods and services required in sub-zero conditions. An emergency in the island of Anguilla in 1969 has procured them a less exacting though not exactly comfortable spell of duty. The island's breakaway from one of the smaller independent groupings into which Britain's former Caribbean possessions had been divided proved to be peaceful and amenable to supervision by a mixed military and police force from England.

That is more than can be said of many other policing actions around the world. In 1963, Naafi was caught up in a general strike in British Guiana (now Guyana) lasting four months. Riots in Cyrenaica were accompanied by a boycott of British ships and assaults on Naafi establishments, in the course of which the Ace of Clubs in Benghazi was burnt to the ground. Shortly before British troops retired from East Africa, they had to deal with emergencies in Tanganyika, Uganda and Zanzibar. Seven hundred troops sent to Swaziland when a crisis threatened, took with them a fourteen day pack prepared by Naafi at less than three hours notice, and a Naafi unit followed to provide a service in the field. The uneasy truce in Cyprus had created enclaves of Greeks and Turks separated by a no-man's-land across which Naafi had to operate at risk. A driver and a storeman were shot dead and seven of the Naafi staff were abducted without trace.

A short and sharp crisis took British troops to Kuwait for four months at the ruler's request, and nineteen Naafi people endured sand storms and bouts of heat exhaustion in their service. They organised a bulk issue store, a canteen, a Services shop and a mobile van to supply the forward units deep in the desert. The troops off duty had the comfort of an air conditioned club run by the four women of the Naafi contingent.

Aden was another hot spot, in both senses of the term, disrupted by strikes and swept by sporadic fighting. There were good clubs and shops in the town, but they were often made inaccessible by a curfew imposed on the districts where Naafi staff lived. Unwary pedestrians were liable to intercept a grenade and casualties were frequent. 'The mortuary is over-worked and full up,' wrote a Naafi official, 'so the resources of the Aden cold store have been enlisted. Room for bodies must be found, food storage takes second place.' In the midst of the terror, that normally bone dry area was hit by freak floods which turned streets into rivers and stretches of desert into lakes: the Naafi bakery was several feet deep in filthy water. Some of the most arduous campaigning took place far from the town of Aden, eight thousand feet up in the Radfan mountains, a four hundred mile haul for the round trip. Aden was evacuated by the British forces late in 1967 and the Naafi bakery kept up its bread round to within forty-eight hours of the end.

Aden profited handsomely (as other territories had done before) from the Naafi presence. When the troops had left, Naafi handed over to the Ministry of Defence properties in Aden valued at nearly £300,000, and these were presented by Her Majesty's Government as a gift to the independent South Arabian administration. Naafi, of course, had to claim reimbursement from HMG.

With the return of the Forces from Aden, Silversands, its idyllic leave centre on the coast of Kenya, lost a larger part of its clientele, though it was retained for sailors in the Beira patrol and British personnel of the three Services attached to the Kenya Forces as trainers and advisers. Guests had private accommodation in the 'bandas' (bungalows), a club with well stocked bar, library, dances, films and stage shows, trips and safaris, and a nursery where children could be safely left in charge of the ayahs while wives joined in the fun.

There was no conflict anywhere on the scale of the Korean war, but the Far East provided its quota of violence. In spite of the pacification, communist guerillas lingered in Malaya and Commonwealth troops and police still had to patrol the jungle paths. Brunei was infested with hit and run rebels and Naafi sent staff, furniture, bedding and vehicles from Singapore for the Forces in that inhospitable territory. They also provided meat pies as a welcome relief from a diet of 'compo' and biscuits, and arranged with a local baker to supply cakes and curry puffs. In the far reaches where Indonesian territory began and border raids were rife, Christmas fare was delivered along with medicines and other non-luxuries by airdrop. Naafi even procured toys for the jungle fighters to send to their children at home. In Kuching Naafi had a large headquarters organisation to serve 10,000 to 15,000 troops deployed over hundreds of miles of rough territory. For a time the trade in Borneo accounted for a large proportion of Naafi's total turnover in the Far East. The takings rose as high as £30,000 a week, and that at duty-free prices.

Military and political actions often affected Naafi when it was not directly involved. The fighting between India and Pakistan in 1965 disrupted the supply line to Nepal, and the diversion of aircraft to help the refugees affected the airlift to the island of Gan. When

Spain closed its frontier with Gibraltar, Naafi had a shortage of fresh vegetables and a staff problem. The Arab-Israeli war in June 1967, which closed the Suez Canal, cut Naafi's communications with the Far East, and trapped in the Canal a ship carrying tinned fruit from Australia to Naafi's base in Cyprus. The separation of Singapore from Malaya brought licensing and other legal complications for Naafi: arrangements had to be made afresh with the new state.

Otherwise Malaya and Singapore provided a colourful and enjoyable domicile for Service men and families. One of the plum Service postings was at Changi, in the north-east of Singapore island, transformed between the wars from a mangrove swamp into a strongpoint guarding the seaward approach to the naval base. At Terendak camp in Malacca, headquarters of the Commonwealth Brigade, Naafi had built beach clubs and, at a cost of a quarter of a million pounds, one of its most ambitious shopping and catering complexes. This included an arcade with grocery shop, central showroom for larger items of household equipment, and hairdressing salon, laundry, watch repairer, shoe repairer, florist and other services let to local concessionaires. A factory building housed cold store, bakery, butchery and milk plant. There was an inn, The Crown, nostalgically decorated with English prints and horse brasses, a club with a barbecue in the centre and a supply of sucking pigs for roasting over the charcoal, and a mobile canteen equipped with bottle cooler to carry iced drinks to soldiers at work in gun parks and training areas, and at play in the swimming pool. The Terendak development was planned for a military township of ten thousand people.

In the far north of Malaya's neighbour, Thailand, Britain and her allies maintained a force to watch for infiltration of communists from over the border in Laos. Naafi ran a Junior Ranks Club staffed by Chinese and an airmen's club for the Royal Australian Air Force. A large airfield was built in appalling conditions on what had once been paddy fields. The dried out paddy fields were covered with eight to ten inches of fine dust, which was churned up by the bulldozers into a choking fog.

Naafi was not simply a squatter in the countries where it attended upon British or NATO Forces. It contributed appreciably to the local economy. Cyprus was a striking example. Naafi bought a third of its local requirements in the island. It encouraged local industry and used its international trading network to export the goods. By this means Cyprus-made socks, stockings and underwear were sold in

North Africa, and Naafi, as export agent, delivered Cyprus wines and fruit squashes to Teheran by RAF plane.

Naafi's reputation was high, even in countries that had no cause to be grateful for its commercial help. A British officer, examining some rings in a jeweller's shop in Ceylon, asked how he could be sure of their quality. 'I would have you know, sir,' said the Ceylonese shopkeeper, 'that we are recommended by Naafi.' For a two-way compliment that would take some beating.

Wherever Naafi has operated abroad, it has had to rely very largely upon local labour. In many places, especially the Middle and Far East, the loyalties that have developed have resulted in many cases of long individual service. The breaking of these ties, when Naafi has had to retire from a country, leaves behind something deeper than unemployment, and Naafi regulars find sadness as well as stimulus in their new posting. One of Naafi's problems during the last stages is to keep the establishments at full strength and efficiency under the cloud of the approaching dissolution. It says much for the good feeling on both sides that the organisation so often holds together until the very end.

Germany continued to be the most tranquil and progressive as well as the largest of Naafi's overseas stations. During the 1960s Naafi's turnover in West Germany and Berlin increased from £17 million to £26 million a year. Seventy family shops served 25,000 Service families. The large supermarket at Rheindahlen took £30,000 a week. Six hundred tons of goods a week poured out of the Krefeld warehouse to shops and clubs throughout the country. The variety of goods available was continually enlarged. The latest fashions were modelled for Service wives, and a mobile display visited those who were far from the shops. Camping equipment and caravans sold well. Trade in band and other musical instruments amounted to some £25,000 a year.

Car hire purchase, introduced by Naafi into Germany in February 1961, proved immediately successful, and agreements with Service men and sponsored civilians soon rose to thirty a month. When the NATO Status of the Forces Supplementary Agreement came into effect on 1st July 1963 about 2,000 Army, RAF and British civilian motorists found their insurance policies invalid in Germany, and for many of them it was a hardship to raise the price (£40 on average) of a new premium. Naafi came to the rescue by arranging immediate cover with a British insurance company for a modest deposit and settlement by instalments, thus spreading the burden most agreeably.

Naafi stirred up local enterprise to help vary the Service man's diet. He missed that succulent vegetable, the marrow, which was unknown to the Germans, and its name absent even from their dictionaries. Naafi taught a German farmer how to grow them; it is not known whether he found customers outside BAOR. There were occasional food crises; one occurred in 1968 when British livestock were devastated by foot and mouth disease and Germany banned meat imports from Britain. In order to save its customers from the disaster of a bangerless dinner, Naafi imported a sausage factory inspector to teach German and Danish producers how to make the British speciality. Customer demand brought another peculiarly British delicacy to the expatriates' tables. A British firm produced a special line of quick frozen crumpets, over a million of which (quick heated) were consumed in one winter alone.

Those problems were easily solved. Much more harassing were the currency changes and the wider issues of Naafi's costs and earnings in Germany. In March 1961 the Deutschemark was revalued upwards, with the result that the conversion rate fell from DM 11.70 to the £ to DM 11.20. To help its customers Naafi increased its rate of discount and rebate immediately by three per cent, and then by a further half per cent when the conversion rate dropped from 11.20 to 11.11. When the conversion rate had settled down, Naafi had to face the long and costly task of re-pricing the thousands of items affected.

In the years that followed, the need to conserve foreign currency, including a reduction in the personal spending of Deutschemarks by Service men and their families, was one of the British government's constant preoccupations. Investigation showed that of some £40 million worth of Deutschemarks drawn each year by the British Forces and their families, about half were spent with Naafi, with philanthropic bodies and Service organisations. Most of this sum flowed back into British channels, but there appeared to be a possibility of diverting a larger slice to Naafi. The Ministry of Defence set up a steering group, with Naafi members, to propose ways of tapping this potential, and a steering group in Germany was set up to give effect to these proposals.

In 1967 the Chancellor of the Exchequer set up a committee to consider further ways of achieving the objective. It was headed by Mr H. Laing, managing director of United Biscuits Limited, with Mr J. A. Lewando, a director of Marks & Spencer Limited, and Mr H. P. T. Prideaux, chairman of Naafi, as the other members. They urged the need for more sales space and a wider range of goods and services in order to divert more Service spending into Naafi shops. The Ministry of Defence responded by releasing twenty-eight shop projects which had been temporarily halted by the financial freeze, and authorised forty-two shop extensions and the creation of a new clothing store at Rheindahlen.

This clothing store, prototype of a very successful development, was planned on Marks & Spencer lines with the co-operation of that company, and was stocked with a wide range of St Michael brand clothes and a large selection produced by other manufacturers. Another major development was the establishment of fifteen butcheries to serve shops throughout the country. Previously, lack of facilities had limited Naafi's retail meat trade to frozen meat imported from the UK and Denmark. Now Naafi shops were better able to compete with German butcher shops. Within a short time sales from the butcheries built up to nearly a million pounds a year.

Further stimulus to Naafi's sales and halting of the Deutschemark drain came from a Buy British campaign, and the organisation of British Weeks in which many British manufacturers, including Naafi's suppliers, participated. Naafi contributed further by providing special catering for these events. The British Week at Gütersloh had, as a grand finale, an RAF At Home, attended by 125,000 people for whom Naafi laid on refreshments. A later air display at Wildenrath drew double that number of spectators for whom Naafi supplied 10,000 beers, 13,000 soft drinks, 50 gallons of tea, 120 gallons of coffee and mountains of sausages, sandwiches and cakes.

The devaluation of the pound in 1967 helped Naafi's sales of UK goods overseas in the long run but precipitated frantic immediate action. Temporary price cuts were introduced almost immediately in family shops and in bars and restaurants in junior ranks' and airmen's clubs, pending the repricing of thousands of lines. Posters, leaflets and forms had to be produced in record time by Naafi's local printing unit at Waldniel. Local paper suppliers ran short of the standard pink paper Naafi used for price reduction forms, and stocks had to be sought in other towns. Five tons of printed matter were split up into ten pound parcels and rushed to shops and clubs. Temporary typists were employed to cope with the paper work. Everywhere, except in Berlin, devaluation cut one sixth off prices. Berlin differed because there the troops were still using a sterling currency (British Armed Forces Special Vouchers) instead of marks; therefore prices remained the same, except for goods from hard currency countries, which cost more.

Two years later, in October 1969, the repricing scramble had to be repeated when Germany again revalued the Deutschemark. All goods imported by Naafi into Germany, that is over seventy per cent of the 18,000 lines stocked, were reduced in price to conform with the new rate of exchange, and again forms, price lists and information leaflets had to be produced at great speed. This time the Krefeld computer helped by recalculating 13,000 prices in four currencies, sterling, francs, marks and guilders. The computer also printed out the master copies of the basic documents, a job completed in less than forty minutes, which would ordinarily have taken six typists three days. But automation has its limitations and the European Service printing unit still had to reproduce from the master sheets 600,000 price alteration forms and price list pages, which had to be collated by non-electronic flesh and blood into sets for every establishment, a task requiring three weeks of twelve hours a day plus weekend working. This was the fifth German currency change to involve Naafi since the Allied armies took over the bankrupt country at the end of the second world war.

Staff shortages have been a constant and acute problem for Naafi as for other traders in Europe. Germany had over-full employment and was importing foreign workers. Naafi looked for recruits in Malta, Spain and Portugal, and appealed to Service wives, sons and daughters to rally round; and asked the Department of Naval Recruiting to tell young men who had failed through, for instance, deficiencies of eyesight to enter the Navy, that a career awaited them in the Naval Canteen Service as canteen assistants and managers. In spite of mechanisation in shops and kitchens, Naafi remained a very human organisation in which for the most part there was no substitute for people.

Some of the difficulties were due to the need to provide services in small isolated outposts that were extravagant of labour. One such community was in Kiel where a minute Naafi shop served twelve British, sixteen American, three French and twenty-five Danish families and provided messing stores for the Kiel Yacht Club. The club's official name proclaimed a less leisured purpose; it was the Army Watermanship Training Centre, a means of fitting landlubbers with sea legs. It formed the British section of a large German naval station on Kiel harbour. Among the shop's customers were Outward Bound training parties en route to Norway and Service men taking part in regular sailing courses. Forty miles away at Putlos another small Naafi shop combined with an airmen's club served twenty-six RAF families. Both shops were stocked by lorry from Krefeld.

Though many Naafi establishments on land were necessarily small and catering for only a handful of people, those serving the Army

and the RAF had all ceased during the 1960s to call themselves canteens. Even in the central organisation where tradition might have
been expected to linger, the term had succumbed to its unfavourable
connotation. The Home Canteen Service became the Home Service,
and the Overseas and European Services were similarly renamed.
But not the Naval Canteen Service. The Navy had clubs and shops
on shore and, after a late start, was following the Army and the
RAF in providing family shopping, but its natural habitat was
afloat, and there the name canteen continued to seem appropriate,
however clublike or shoplike the Naafi corner might be.

What a tight corner it is in some ships! In a frigate, even the
installation of a vending machine has to be worked out in inches.
The machines may be landed on deck by helicopter but have to be
manhandled below. This is difficult enough in an aircraft carrier but
in a small ship it has sometimes meant cutting away part of a hatch-
way to admit one machine. The vending machine is a welcome
adjunct to the small ship's canteen, where the total Naafi complement
is often only one man. It is useful also in a large ship where there
will be anything from five to fifteen Naafi men serving up to 2,000
customers; not only handing out small everyday consumables but
now also taking orders for durables such as refrigerators, food
mixers and washing machines for the naval man to send home to
his wife.

In new ships under construction, Naafi helps to plan the canteen.
A Naafi representative goes on board to 'line out' the space allocated
to the canteen; that is, to paint on the empty floor and walls the
outline of the basic fittings and equipment – counter, display shelves,
refrigerator and so on. The siting of the vending machines presents
complications which are unknown on land, such as the effects of
pitch and roll, high temperatures and variations in the electrical
supply and water pressure. The most up to date ships have air
conditioned canteens.

The provisioning of ships' canteens can still be a nightmare for
Naafi in spite of modernisation. On one occasion, HMS *Eagle*,
berthed in Singapore, required to be restocked in thirty-six hours
with goods brought from a warehouse nineteen miles away and filling
40,000 cases. At the same time the harassed Naafi staff had to top up
a Royal Fleet Auxiliary vessel with 13,000 cases of goods. The RFA
ships are floating warehouses, and six of the forty-two in service
carry Naafi stores. Goods are stacked on pallets below deck and
moved by forklift truck as in any shore warehouse. The purpose is
replenishment of ships at sea; some of the warehouse ships have

helicopter flight decks, hangars and workshops to facilitate 'Vertrep' – vertical replenishment – during which the receiving ship can remain fully operational.

In recent years the Navy has been building large housing estates for the families, to which Naafi has contributed modern shopping facilities. One of these is the Churchill Estate at Helensburgh, home of the submarine crews at Faslane, where Britain's Polaris and conventional submarines are based. The social and shopping centre comprises a supermarket on the new Naafi pattern, selling all kinds of goods from ice lollies and cornflakes to postage stamps and motor tyres, and a community centre, the Drumfork Club – named after the neighbouring burn and not the cutlery. The Faslane base has the Trident Club, with large lounge, three bars, games room and television room; and a shopping arcade containing a Services shop, bookstall, post office, men's wear and sports gear shop, barber and a reception point for laundry and dry cleaning.

Naafi as shopkeeper gradually took the lead from Naafi as caterer during the Corporation's fifth decade. This was one of the main features of the reorientation of the service in response to changes in the character and deployment of the armed forces. It was also an element in Naafi's successful trading during the 1960s. Though the Forces became more exacting in their requirements as they shrank in numbers, Naafi's turnover rose year after year. From £58½ million in 1960-61 it had mounted to £82 million by 1969, a substantial increase even allowing for inflation.

How was it done? The simple answer would be, by sound business management, but that is compounded of many different skills. Marketing has played an important part by studying demand and meeting the competition with acceptable prices and customer incentives. Procedures have been modernised with the aid of computers and other forms of office automation and with mechanical handling in warehouses. Work study and organisation and methods have improved productivity; training and fringe benefits have raised staff competence and morale. Old buildings, difficult to run efficiently, have been replaced with new ones; the warehouse at Amesbury, still being enlarged, embodies the latest ideas in storage and distribution. Behind all these activities is a strong central administration, experienced in financial management and in all branches of Naafi's operation, and keeping personally in touch with people and events wherever the Naafi service extends.

Progress must not only be made but proclaimed. Naafi used public relations before most businesses had heard of the term.

J

Since 1941 when the late Claude F. Luke became press officer and in recent years under Mr R. C. McKechney as chief public relations officer, the function of communication with the Corporation's customers and the external public has grown in scope and sophistication. The information material that goes out from Imperial Court, and the PR spokesmen who tour the British regions and the overseas stations to explain Naafi's purpose and activities, are having some effect in bringing the image of Naafi up to date. Though music hall jokes persist, the press is beginning to discuss Naafi seriously, like any other business. It starts its second half century with enhanced prestige and with much cause for confidence, but also with some old and new problems for which there will be no simple solution.

CHAPTER SIX

Today and Tomorrow

To those who knew Naafi when it dished out beer and buns in scruffy barrack canteens, its progress in fifty years would look miraculous. The present board take a more realistic view: if Naafi had not been capable of such improvement it would not have survived to celebrate its Jubilee. As the pace of change in Britain's armed forces quickens, the management are asking some searching questions about the adequacy of Naafi's contribution. How well does it serve current needs? Where could it be improved? Is it flexible enough to adjust to any new pattern of national defence?

Before those questions can be considered, it might be useful to sketch a portrait of Naafi as it looks on its fiftieth birthday. It is a large business; not as big as the giants in catering and retailing, but comparable with companies in the rank immediately below. It sells goods and services currently to the value of over £80 million a year and shows a creditable surplus of about £4½ million. Since it is owned and controlled by the Services and has no other shareholders, the whole of the profit is used for the benefit of the customer and the development of the business. £3¾ million was returned to the Services in the form of rebates, discounts and other benefits in 1969.

The money is handed back at different times as well as in different forms. Each month the canteens and clubs return five per cent of the takings to the ships' and units' welfare funds, irrespective of whether the canteens and clubs are run at a profit or a loss. The customer can see the amount posted on a notice board. But that is only a portion of the benefit. On every cash purchase in the family shops the customer receives a five per cent discount or, in the UK and Germany, the equivalent in dividend stamps, whichever is preferred. A similar discount is paid in the Services shops on any single item (except cigarettes and tobacco) costing ten shillings or more: on all other purchases rebate is paid into the unit funds. At the end of Naafi's financial year, what is left after providing for reserves is paid to the Services as extra rebate. In fifty years Naafi has distributed over

£165 million to its customers in rebates, dividends and discounts.

Because of its peculiar obligations – to provide a service even at a loss if required, and to distribute a rebate before a profit has been earned – Naafi is granted certain rights by the Ministry of Defence. Among them is that of exclusive trading in Service barracks, stations and camps, and Her Majesty's ships. In effect, the concession is not strictly exclusive; some philanthropic bodies and traders have the privilege of competing. Nowhere else does Naafi come anywhere near to being a monopoly, except in remote places where no competitor would find it worth while to intrude.

Since the armed forces are widely scattered, Naafi serves them through a large number of comparatively small outlets. The catering side runs 605 clubs, including canteens aboard Her Majesty's ships, 90 mobile canteens, and in some places central clubs for officers and other ranks. The distributive trade is handled by 510 family shops and mobile shops, and 260 Services shops. Auxiliary services include petrol stations and bowling alleys, hire purchase, mail order and gift parcel schemes, insurance and unit trusts, and special catering for unit and other private functions.

Naafi employs about 19,000 men and women, and runs nearly 1,500 road vehicles, in its worldwide operation. For its overseas Service customers it exports goods to the value of over £12 million a year. It owns warehouses and stores, sausage factories and bakeries; it blends and packages tea and coffee, bottles wines and fruit drinks, manufactures mineral waters, produces printed matter and personal stationery for the Forces.

In brief, Naafi is club operator, wholesaler, retailer, manufacturer and exporter, a combination which is unique in British trade. No ordinary grocery chain or department store runs clubs, no other retailer has an arbitrarily restricted clientele, no other commercial organisation is required to provide unprofitable services. Naafi's basic terms of reference remain unchanged, no matter how it evolves as a business.

The variety and complexity of this business, coupled with its singleness of purpose as 'the Forces' Co-operative', necessitates a strong central organisation. The headquarters costs are comparatively heavy, but decentralisation would merely transfer the cost to the periphery and weaken the board's control. Their obligation to support Service welfare funds out of the trading surplus makes them particularly cost conscious and sensitive to criticism on grounds of economy. A feature which is rare in a business of this size is the compactness of the top executive management. When the chairman relinquished his executive duties he reverted to the old Naafi tradition that the chair should be an unpaid office. This has left a paid executive board of only three persons, Mr E. W. Mac-Gowan, OBE, as chief executive, flanked by Mr C. A. Layard, OBE, and Mr J. E. Ellison, FCA, who share responsibility for the executive departments.

Like the managing director, the two executive directors are Naafi products. Mr Layard came to the board in 1964 via the management of the Naval Canteen Service and then of the Home Service; Mr Ellison in 1968 through accounts and supplies. Mr Layard's official title is merchandise director, but in Naafi's vocabulary the term is a portmanteau containing not only buying, marketing, retailing, automatic vending and special catering, but also bakeries and meat factories, club development, staff training and the Forces Press. Mr Ellison, officially administrative director, describes his own sphere as 'the grey area between merchandising on the one side and nothing on the other'. Gathered under his umbrella, in addition to the central administrative and the support services, are audit and credit, insurance, property and building, the technical aspects of transport, and the personnel, medical and public relations departments. Obviously the responsibilities of the two executive directors overlap in almost every department. A warehouse is a structure as well as a store, a club uses equipment and also sells goods. The two directors would often have difficulty in defining the boundary where the one stopped and the other started, but they work in partnership without having to argue about prerogatives.

One reason why executive control can be left in so few hands at the top is the support that the directors receive from a corps of highly experienced managers in the trading and specialised departments. Most of them have come to headquarters through the rigours of work in the field, some of it during the second world war. No one administering a branch of the service, or a function, or a group of establishments, or even working under a pile of paper, can remain mentally desk-bound if at some time he has landed on an enemy-held coast wearing the EFI uniform, fixed up a bulk issue store in the jungle, managed a club in the desert, sold cornflakes and washing powder to Service wives, organised supplies for ships' canteens at sea or in port.

Another source of strength for the executive board is the part played by the five non-executive directors. These are high ranking businessmen, part time and unpaid members of the board of management, who bring to the Corporation's counsels experience of trading in all the fields covered by the Naafi service. Sir Charles Hardie, CBE, FCA, the deputy chairman, is chairman of BOAC, of the British Printing Corporation and of the Metropolitan Estate and Property Corporation, and is a practising chartered accountant. He is Naafi's authority on finance and the City. Mr C. H. W. Troughton, CBE, MC, TD, is chairman of W. H. Smith & Son Limited whose problems in managing a large chain of retail shops have affinities with those of Naafi. Mr K. L. Hall, as a director of Trust House Fortes Limited and of Kardomah Limited, is an expert in catering. Mr B. A. Stapleton, OBE, MC, TD, is assistant managing director of Lewis's Limited, the group which includes Selfridges, and understands the retailing of a variety of merchandise including consumer durables. Mr J. D. Spooner, FCA, the board's latest and youngest member, has interests in textiles, timber, property and furniture.

The non-executive directors attend the monthly board meetings with their executive colleagues. They contribute ideas and opinions, exert a balancing influence on board decisions, and keep Naafi's interests in mind when engaged on other than Naafi business. They also serve on two Naafi sub-committees, one on the Corporation's investments and the other on salaries for the more senior executive staff.

Their work for Naafi is disinterested: like many leaders of public companies they are glad to give part of their time to a cause of national importance. The benefit is not, however, all one way. Naafi has much to teach as well as to learn. In an interview published in *Accountancy Age* early in 1970, Sir Charles Hardie is quoted as saying: 'I think one of the most significant appointments I got was soon after the war, when I became deputy chairman of the Naafi ... This gave me an insight into running a large business, and I think the Naafi is the best run business that I am connected with, without question. It has the advantage of being commercially angled but with the great influence of Service administration, which is so superior to anything you ever find in industry.'

Outside opinion is all the more important to Naafi because it lacks the criteria that the share market brings to bear upon public companies. It has no Stock Exchange quotation to act as a barometer of progress, and since it is a Services utility operating 'not for profit', growth is a less reliable measure of success than it would be for a purely commercial enterprise, though Naafi is growing and must grow in order to maintain its service. It has to rely more than most businesses upon intangible indicators – the grumblings of soldiers, the attitude of shoppers, the patronage of the clubs, and the management's awareness of social change. At the same time, Naafi has to accept conditions imposed by events which no one can control and by official decrees which are as inexorable as those of the Medes and Persians, and has to devise adjustments which will prove to be a positive gain rather than simply a compensation for loss.

That positive attitude has motivated the structural, organisational and procedural changes that have become necessary as Naafi approached its fiftieth birthday. The most compelling cause has been the reduction in number and size of its overseas interests. Apart from a toehold in Kenya, Africa is lost to Naafi: its profitable trading in Cyrenaica ceased in 1970. Naafi remains active in Gibraltar and Cyprus, to a diminishing extent in Malta, and in a small way in Sardinia; east of Suez in Masirah, Bahrein, Sharjah, Mauritius, Gan, Thailand, Borneo, Hong Kong and, less certainly, in Malaysia and Singapore; and across the Atlantic in British Honduras and Bermuda. Party politics and the strength of the national economy will determine whether, and to what extent, Britain retains defence commitments in the Far East, though the Navy will still be there. Otherwise, the armed forces have ebbed into Europe, where as far as one can see Nato forces will remain, with a large UK contingent.

Trouble could no doubt still arise in politically unstable countries, requiring the assistance of British forces with Naafi at their elbow, but it is likely to be a fairly rare event. The last alert was in Libya in 1969, when the deposition of King Idris created an ominous situation, but serious civil disturbance was avoided. It is possible that most countries will in future prefer to organise their own fire brigades rather than invite outside help. Life is going to be less exciting, but safer for Naafi's employees.

The narrowing of the nation's defence obligations will no doubt help the economy, but it means that Naafi's revenue will be harder earned. Overseas markets have always been more profitable than those at home. Away from home, the troops and their families converge on Naafi, where the language and the merchandise are familiar and British insularity can be indulged. In the UK those incentives are absent and competition from native suppliers and amenities is therefore stronger. The abandonment of overseas stations involves the repatriation of Naafi's customers to England where, instead of being concentrated in a military cantonment with Naafi on their doorstep, they tend to be dispersed through the country, often in places where Naafi shops and clubs are less accessible than those of competitors. So more and more of Naafi's business is being diverted to its least profitable sector.

The repercussions are being felt throughout the Naafi organisation. In 1969 it was decided to split the overgrown Home Service into two departments, a North and a South, each headed by a departmental manager. Other changes coincided. The trading departments, all of them except European Service based at the London headquarters, had always had their own administrative sections. Now it was decided to centralise the support services in order to relieve the departmental heads of a load of chores which had tended to absorb energies better spent on the trading function. The result has been a more rational division of work and a more economical use of human resources.

The duties thus relinquished were transferred to a new department named Central Administrative Services. This department also took over much of the administrative burden from the Naval Canteen Service as far as the special circumstances of the Navy would permit. The marketing department was extended; a special branch was formed to handle club development and automatic vending; credit and audit services were departmentalised and so was transport. The top management looked at the headquarters activities with a fresh eye, tidied and oiled the machinery, rearranged functions into logical groups, and produced an organisation better fitted to take the strains that new defence policies might impose.

The weight of responsibility carried by the headquarters organisation had caused increasing congestion, which the removal of some departments to the building in Kennings Way had not done enough to relieve. The Kennings Way building had become overdue for replacement, and towards the end of the 1960s the management made plans to dispose of the site, transfer its warehousing and manufacturing functions to the new central warehouse complex at Amesbury, and erect an office building designed by Naafi's architect on a site acquired at Kennington Cross, where Kennington Road and Kennington Lane meet. Excavation is in progress as Naafi celebrates its Jubilee.

One can hardly dig a spadeful of earth in London without revealing historical remains; and this site has yielded a richer archaeological reward than most. The Southwark and Lambeth Archaeological Society, who spent sixteen months excavating adjacent land, uncovered the ground plans of the fourteenth century palace of the Black Prince. There was a hall 82 feet by 50 feet, with the Prince's chamber at one end, and at the other a parlour, a private chapel and the remains of a tower. The kitchens and stables had occupied the plot where Naafi's new building will stand. The palace was demolished by order of Henry VIII in 1531, and the Long Barn, famous for its vast size, which was built on the land, incorporated what remained of the stables. The searchers also uncovered the foundations of a manor house erected later on the site. Among objects unearthed by the dig were six jettons or counters used for calculation six hundred years before Naafi brought its accounting machines and computers to the manor of Kennington. A more sinister discovery was the skeleton of a young man. 'From the unusual angle in which the remains were lying,' said Mr G. Dawson, vice-chairman of the society, 'we deduced that it had been an irregular burial.'

When the new headquarters has been built, it will take over all the clerical operations now housed in Kennings Way, and enough from Imperial Court to give elbow room to the remaining staff. For many years Kennings Way was Naafi's only general warehouse in the UK. It still handles non-foods, such as sports goods, gifts and durables; also tea and coffee packaging and wine bottling; and the export department which makes up and dispatches the smaller consignments overseas. All these activities will be transferred to the new centre for general goods (ie groceries and provisions) at Amesbury. Other food warehouses in the Naafi chain are at Darlington, Portsmouth and Devonport; there are produce warehouses at Spitalfields, near the market, and at Aldershot and Edinburgh; also a fish buying office at Grimsby, three bakeries and three sausage factories. In addition, Naafi has warehouses handling furniture and furnishings, kitchen and display equipment, tableware and cutlery.

Those serve the home territory only. In Germany Naafi has a central warehouse at Krefeld, a sports and camping warehouse, two produce warehouses, three bakeries, two mineral water factories and an equipment warehouse. There are warehouses in Gibraltar, Malta, Cyprus, Bahrein, Singapore and Hong Kong; bakeries in Cyprus, Malta and Singapore, and an export warehouse in Hong Kong. At sea Naafi has the use of eight stores supply ships.

The warehouses and the transport activities in the UK have been the scene of Naafi's latest experiments in productivity. Staff shortage and high wages have forced upon Naafi, as upon all businesses, the need to recruit wisely and encourage effort with incentives. In co-operation with outside consultants Naafi has applied work study techniques to the warehousing and distribution routines. It was necessary to explain to the staff the painless nature of the operation. There is a long-standing belief among employees throughout industry that the work study expert stands over you with a stop watch in one hand and a whip in the other, like an overseer in the old plantations. What he has done in fact at Naafi has been to determine a standard of performance upon which to base an incentive bonus. Standards have been set for various operations – goods received, storage, picking, assembly and dispatch – and rewards paid for exceeding the basic effort. At the same time work has been lightened, movement accelerated and muscle saved, by providing workers with the most up to date mechanical aids. The result has been very successful: reduced costs for the organisation and a better deal for its workers.

Following research by Naafi's own organisation and methods specialists, work study is now being applied to the clerical departments. Here the performance has to be appraised on a group scale (group capacity assessment in the jargon of business consultancy) and not on individual achievement. It is based on the findings of a clerical work measurement programme. The group activity is broken down into measurable units, the average time required for each unit of work is determined, and the figure is multiplied by the flow of these unit jobs through the office, allowing for time lost through sickness, holidays and the smaller normal interruptions. The result indicates the number of staff required to perform the function, and provides guidance on more effective deployment of staff. The system pinpoints duplication of work or other waste effort, and may reveal the causes of fluctuations in work flow and the way to iron them out.

The full implementation of the programme may take up to three years. It will be costly, especially because senior staff seconded to the operation are denied for the time to other departments. But the economy will be substantial in the end. Associated with the efficiency drive are highly sophisticated machines and systems. These include electronic calculating machines on mobile trolleys, an automatic coin sorter, an automatic typewriter working from punched tape, a telex link for communication with the overseas establishments, a microfilm recorder which transfers up to 2,500 invoices on to a single 100 foot reel of 16 mm film; and of course the computers.

A computer is not only an office utility but a catalyst, demanding special conditions for its efficient application and producing changes in the organisation. Some users of computers in industry and commerce have been disappointed with the results obtained, mainly because they have not prepared the ground adequately or have failed to make full use of this expensive instrument. Naafi has avoided those mistakes. Savings attributable to the computer are already substantial, and will fully recoup development costs by 1971.

While office automation saves manpower, it requires a higher standard of training and skill in those who have to control operations. Naafi is proud of its staff training. At Wingham, its training centre at Claygate, Surrey, all grades of staff receive instruction, from induction courses for newcomers to grooming for shop and club management and refreshers for established managers. Training is based on action rather than talk; bar assistants serve behind a bar and learn how to do such jobs as cleaning out the beer pipes; kitchen staff get their training in a fully equipped kitchen; shop assistants have to handle a simulated awkward customer; clerical workers use the actual documents in realistic situations; projects such as setting up a service point for an open air event are completed, then pulled to pieces verbally and physically and reconstructed on improved lines. The instructors have had long service with Naafi in many capacities and countries, and everything they teach has been learnt in the field. They keep up to date by themselves taking refresher courses.

Wingham takes charge of training up to district manager level. Senior officials are sent for training or refresher courses to appropriate outside colleges such as the Administrative Staff College at Henley. Apart from formal tuition, which is necessarily brief, people learn their skills on the job. One of Wingham's most valuable services is to teach managers how to train their subordinates.

The training of shop and club staff is particularly important to Naafi. Since Naafi belongs to its customers, it depends even more than other shopkeepers upon the quality of those who represent it at the point of sale. There is a double problem: like all retailers and caterers, and in spite of self-service and vending machines, Naafi remains 'labour intensive', that is, the number of employees is fairly high in relation to turnover; but it is at the humblest level of employment that Naafi comes into closest contact with its customers. To most of the people who use Naafi's services, Naafi is a shop assistant, a cashier, a barmaid, a delivery man; and it is upon their competence, conduct and personality that Naafi is judged. The strength of the Naafi chain thus depends upon its weakest links, and that presents a problem, however good the links may be of their kind. It is complicated by the tendency in the country as a whole for standards to fall, and the recruitment of good types is becoming more and more difficult in a branch of employment which is not among the most popular. Naafi studies rates of pay in other organisations in order to keep its own competitive. One important incentive it cannot usually offer is, of course, employment in a busy town centre.

Another problem of Naafi's retail business is that of reconciling the need for variety of goods and services with the hard fact of inadequate premises. The Forces are scattered over the home territory in small units and Naafi must follow suit. But the customers want department store choice, and a miniature department store is a contradiction in terms. The shops cannot accommodate the required stocks, and can show no more than a token display of the larger and more expensive goods. Some of the results are surprising; the supermarket at Tidworth has shown, among the washing machines, refrigerators, men's shirts and pants, a motor car labelled with the name of the local dealer from whom it could be purchased on Naafi hire purchase terms.

The strain on the shop manager is considerable. In addition to discounts and dividends on every ordinary purchase, he has to cope with telephone orders and with deliveries, deposit accounts, instalment credit, cash on delivery and hire purchase; has to be prepared to handle messing supplies and cellar accounts. Many of the shops, in the UK particularly, are so small that it is not feasible to provide a fully qualified assistant, though the manager gets maximum support from Naafi supervisors and from the latest aids to shopkeeping. The problem would be solved if the Services were to be concentrated into fewer and larger communities; then Naafi could similarly rationalise its network of shops and reduce the number of unprofitable outlets as the commercial chains are doing. The Forces have their own problems; they find it difficult to get enough married quarters in the desired locations to make concentration possible. There is good reason to hope that the situation will change in the course of the deployment of the Forces and their families in the UK after the current rundown. When the long term pattern emerges it may be found that the State has been able to form compact married quarter colonies which would enable the occupants to get full advantage from their own shopping service.

Meanwhile, in spite of the limitations, Naafi's shops are on the whole a fairly profitable department of the business. It employs modern business methods in order to improve its competitive position in the retail jungle. The shopping basket test already described, whereby Naafi keeps a continuous watch on the prevailing prices of standard groups of goods, enables Naafi to strike an average which, when discount or dividend has been deducted, is the lowest in the market. This price advantage is apparent to the more observant customer but not easy to convey generally throughout the Services. The myth persists in some quarters that it costs more to shop at Naafi than in the popular chains. Many of Naafi's home customers still do their main shopping in the High Street and use the

Naafi shop as the village store. But the economy of shopping with Naafi, together with such facilities as deliveries and credit terms which the chains do not offer, are becoming more widely known and appreciated.

In shop organisation, as well as service to the customer Naafi has introduced changes which put it well to the front in retail trading economy. One of the time consuming activities in most grocers' shops is the random replenishment of the shelves as the goods are sold. A work study team appointed by Naafi's organisation and methods experts found that in one week the random topping up of shelves in a shop that stocked some 12,000 items involved the staff in 1,731 trips between storeroom and the point of sale, and consumed 112 manhours of work, equal to the work of three assistants. In order to save much of the leg work and all the incidental muddle, the O and M (since rechristened research and development) department has devised an original system called 'aid-to-refill' (ATR). When fully in operation it cuts the number of manhours to thirty-eight.

ATR is a system based on the weekly sales of each line over a six months period, allowing for staff absences, seasonal fluctuations and other variables. It provides the manager with two visible records, one of which controls the shelf refill level and the other the re-stocking requirements. He is thus able to review every line daily, and ensure a continuous flow of goods into the shopping area without overstocking in the storeroom. Though method is ultimately much easier to cope with than confusion, its adoption disturbs old notions and upsets cherished, if inefficient, procedures. Some shops take longer to systematise than others, but it is a remarkable fact that some of the most enthusiastic users of ATR are among the older managers.

Naafi has the advantage over other British retail organisations that it has a flourishing overseas trade. In Britain the Service men and their families can shop around and are not dependent on Naafi, but they tend to cling to Naafi abroad. In Britain the Naafi management often wonder whether they are carrying diversification too far, whether they are in danger of forgetting that they are primarily grocers, but in Germany diversification is a necessary part of the service to a clientele in exile. It has a price advantage which is a strong attraction: the goods are free of British purchase tax and the saving is, of course, passed on to the customer. Germany will remain, in many respects, a case apart. Compared with Germany, civilian clothes and fashion goods are a very small part of Naafi's business in the UK, restricted mainly to underwear, leisure wear and such oddments as braces and belts. The Service wife with BAOR shops readily in Naafi's Marks & Spencer type of store or buys clothing on mail order through Naafi from Littlewood's catalogue.

On the retail side Naafi has developed into a mature and well organised business, packing a remarkably varied range of goods and services into its restricted sphere of operation as the Services retailer. A few additions to the list may still be possible: launderettes have been tried experimentally but unsuccessfully, dry cleaning installations have been considered, so have holiday services and estate agency; but the board have to look very carefully into the economics of lateral expansion, and avoid anything that might detract from the primary function of supplying customers, in the UK particularly, with their day to day requirements of foods and household goods. Naafi's future expansion will be mainly vertical, selling more of the same merchandise to the same customers. Between 1969 and 1970 there has been a satisfactory increase in the total volume of Naafi's business. Sales rose 7.3 per cent despite a 3.6 per cent drop in the number of customers, and purchases per head increased from 82s 8d to 92s, a rise of 11.3 per cent.

One direction in which Naafi believes it could increase its service with benefit to its own trading and to the customer is in the provision of supplies for messing both in the UK and overseas. Since a larger proportion of Service men will in future be joined by their families, their use of the dining hall will tend to decrease, and it would seem reasonable and economical to transfer the responsibility for supplying the diminished volume of messing goods from the public purse into Naafi channels. Naafi already has to distribute food, including a substantial element of the messing requirement, to all Service locations at home and overseas, and could therefore take this addition to its volume of sales in its stride. The increased financial rewards this could bring would of course help the Service welfare funds. While this possible development is being considered by the Ministry of Defence, it indicates that the opportunity to make more use of Naafi's organisation and accumulated skills may not have been sufficiently explored by the Services, and that necessary changes in the Naafi service can be concurrent with and need not lag behind those in the armed forces.

There are no acute problems in Naafi's supply and distribution services: its big problem, however, is the club. The social club concept has fitted more comfortably into Naval and Air Force life than into that of the Army. It is possible that Naafi has not taken sufficiently into account the different organisation and needs of the soldier. The Navy and the RAF are generally organised on a station instead of a unit basis. They are physically more static than the Army, and better able, therefore, to develop a social life with the club as its centre. There is a co-operative spirit, which expresses itself in active club committees, a keen attendance and the organising of entertainments, often on an ambitious scale.

The Army officially adopted the social club principle and provided funds to convert existing clubs and build new ones to the same standard. This new club concept would seem admirably fitted for large army communities such as ordnance depots. But Naafi is largely concerned with individual battalions, regiments and other units which move round fairly frequently and are often out on training exercises. Moreover, a particular camp may sometimes contain several units from different arms of the Service, each with its own ideas about community life, but all sharing the one Naafi club. In those circumstances it is not so easy for commanding officers to develop their club on the same social lines as clubs in large static camps, however much they may wish to do so. The units' mobility, the time factor and, not least, the relatively small number of potential club members, all present obstacles.

There is another stumbling block to the fullest development of the social club – the strong feeling which has always existed, particularly in operational units and their training depots, that the junior NCO, having achieved this important milestone in his career, should be accorded suitable privileges, among them a separate bar in the club. Such accommodation has always been provided by the State, and it often means that Naafi has to staff a separate and – since a large proportion of men live out nowadays – quite uneconomic service point in the interests of segregation.

From a commercial point of view this is not a happy situation for Naafi; indeed, if the Army were to insist on separate junior NCOs' messes, the club system could break down altogether. Naafi realises that it is in no position to change long standing military traditions, and takes account of the wishes of individual unit commanders while continuing to promote and extend the social club concept.

Separateness is not only a matter of ranking. Even individual barracks can form separate clans, difficult to break up and re-form into larger, less exclusive groupings. That may be the main reason why some Army units form splinter clubs. These may be started by a 'tea wallah' with an urge to try his hand at catering, and settle into a narrow fraternity. Some of the amateur caterers get into difficulties and ask Naafi to take them over. None can offer the amenities of the Naafi social club. But some commanding officers, especially in Germany, encourage these break-away clubs on the grounds that they foster company, squadron or battery spirit and keep the troops off the streets. Naafi has asked the Army department of the Ministry of Defence whether it intends to 'legitimise' the splinter clubs, and if so what their relation to Naafi will be. They are undoubtedly a retrograde step, but also a portent. Their existence and acceptability reveals a weakness in Naafi: it has not found a social formula or achieved sufficient flexibility to suit the Army: it has not completely fulfilled its original obligation, as Sir John Fortescue has expressed it, 'to be all things to all fighting men'.

In the process of evolving from the primitive barrack canteen, the club has become demilitarised; a place where the member can escape temporarily into a civilian type of environment. But in doing so it has set itself the difficult task of sustaining a dual identity. During working hours it is something between a snack bar and the better type of industrial canteen, sparsely patronised but requiring to be staffed to serve whoever may drop in. At night it must be capable of transformation into a place of recreation and entertainment, where a man can get a game or a dance, enjoy a show or sit with his friends over a drink, quietly or noisily as he feels inclined. This dual character is not easy or economical to support, and it is not surprising that many of the clubs are run at a loss.

The Naafi management regard the provision of suitable recreational facilities for all the Services as a problem in sociology. They are looking at the highly successful working men's clubs where there is a warm human feeling, a sense of fellowship and participation, a relaxed and congenial atmosphere offering escape from work and worry. The circumstances differ from those of the armed forces and the pattern cannot be copied; but vocational differences do not obscure the fact that the young Service men are a cross section of the youth of the country, with similar tastes and recreational needs. Naafi wants to know not only whether its clubs, even at their best, are what the young Service man wants today, but whether they will meet the demands of tomorrow – as far as one can guess what Service life will be like in the near future.

Much depends on what the Ministry of Defence decides should be the character of national defence and the kind of fighting man needed. Will the Services become a close community, a corps of picked men, dedicated to their calling and willing to seek their social satisfaction as well as their professional career within the citadel?

Previous page: Naafi Headquarters, Imperial Court, London
Naafi catering at the Akrotiri water-ski club, Cyprus
Olympic Club serves the men and women of the British Military Headquarters in Berlin

*During the day the Naafi shop is the main attraction at Summit
House Club, Berlin, which also provides an evening rendezvous
for Servicemen*

Marlborough Club, Rhine Army, Rheindahlen, West Germany

An English country pub in the heart of beer-keller land, Cavendish Arms at Barker Barracks, Paderborn, Germany

Windmill Hill social club commands a magnificent view of Gibraltar Harbour and the coast of Spain

Naafi mobile canteen serves the Royal Navy

Shopping centre, RAF Marham, Norfolk
The greengrocery, Naafi supermarket, Tidworth, Wiltshire

Supermarket at Aldershot, Hampshire

Naafi warehouse, Amesbury, Wiltshire. It stocks over £1,000,000 of goods in 116,000 sq ft of storage space which is currently being extended to 217,000 sq ft

The concept of the armed forces as a race apart would be novel and revolutionary in our society, going against the general trend towards uniformity, perhaps demanding special methods of recruitment and screening, and using other incentives than those which apply to civilian occupations. The Naafi club would be an important feature of the new conditions, planned to serve an exacting and self-sufficient clientele.

If on the other hand the new defence forces are to be an open instead of a close community, sharing their social life with the civilian population and admitting civilians into the military sanctum, the Naafi club will have to be even more competitive with public entertainment and amenity, or it will die of neglect. Whichever type of community the Services decide upon, there will be two essential requirements in the social clubs: they must be as free from restrictions and institutionalism as the 'local', and the members must be encouraged to co-operate in organising a full programme of good entertainment. The club will really have proved itself when the Service man has come to regard it as his club rather than Naafi's. It should be the kind of club for which a man does not need to apologise, but where he feels he can take his girl with confidence and even pride.

As always, the Services must call the tune and Naafi must play the instrument well. Its performance has improved enormously in the last decade. It is much more adaptable, more amenable to new ideas and appreciative of modern techniques, better equipped structurally and administratively to face any emergency. It continues, by skilled management, to prosper in trading circumstances which are among the most difficult in its history apart from war. Whatever drastic changes may be required of Naafi in the future, it will no doubt continue to be a necessary and profitable servant of the Services.

K

Postscript

By Edward MacGowan, managing director, NAAFI

It is right that at the close of our first fifty years' service we in Naafi should look behind us down the years, not merely in admiration of the splendid work and achievements of our predecessors, but in self-criticism to see where history may show that our policies or practices were not ideal, so that if possible we can improve our performance in the future.

More fundamentally, it is right too that we should review our origins and even the very reasons for our existence, to be sure that our organisation is essential to the wellbeing of Her Majesty's Forces and that it is meeting their requirements in the best way possible.

Naafi and its predecessors sprang from the loins of the industrial revolution just as surely as did the co-operative movement itself. In the latter years of the nineteenth century the poor and ignorant children of that revolution – and the Service men were no different – were often exploited ruthlessly by the tradesmen, whether they were in the High Street or were the contractors operating the canteens. Such exploitation is recorded in humorous verse of the time:

> 'The hell-instructed grocer
> Has a temple made of tin,
> And the ruin of good innkeepers
> Is loudly urged therein;
> But now the sands are running out
> From sugar of a sort,
> The grocer trembles; for his time,
> Just like his weight, is short.'

Our predecessor, the Canteen and Mess Co-operative Society, was the Services' answer.

It could be said truly that this type of exploitation does not exist today, though it is inherent in a system in which every private trader seeks to maximise his profits. But whenever a trader is serving a comparatively remote community his prices will tend to be high as he exploits his monopoly. Thus, although the poor and ignorant Service man no longer exists, the possibility of his exploitation or that of his family certainly does exist. And against this Naafi is his safeguard.

Moreover, that other justification of the co-operative movement, the enjoyment by its members of the net profits derived from trading with themselves must, it seems to me, continue to be applicable to the Naafi movement; the generation of funds for the private purposes of the Services, whether as individuals or as units, must surely always be preferable to a system under which the profit derived from the Services' spendings goes into the private pockets of civilian traders.

Thus the continuing need for Naafi seems to me to be totally justified, and we are left only with the question of how best we can provide these dual interests of the Forces: the services which they need and the private spending money they want.

One lesson at least we shall learn from our predecessors; like them we shall seek continually to improve and refine our service in clubs and shops, and in supplies for units and messes, so that standards are maintained which match those of the very best in the civilian world. Moreover we shall pursue vigorously any possible means by which we can profitably and to the advantage of our customers increase our participation in those fields in which we are already established, while seeking to develop our trade in other fields.

The car hire purchase scheme is already an established success, and various schemes for insurance and savings are already well launched. Others will follow. These efforts, coupled with close attention to our internal efficiency and continued employment of the latest techniques and aids to productivity, will maintain a prosperous organisation based on a contented, prosperous and therefore efficient staff.

It must never be forgotten that Naafi serves the Services in war as well as in peace and that this too provides an essential motive for its existence. Hope and pray as we must for lasting peace, Naafi, like the Services, must be prepared for wars, large or small, hot or cold, cataclysmic or conventional. We shall continue to concentrate – uncommercial as the obligation is – on this preparedness, so that, should the occasion unhappily arise, we shall be able to give at least as good an account of ourselves as did our predecessors.

AUTHOR'S ACKNOWLEDGEMENTS

There are so few published references to Naafi, apart from the Corporation's own publications and occasional news items in the press, that I am grateful for material from Monica Baldwin's autobiography *I Leap Over the Wall, We Also Serve* by Doris Pilkington, *The Forgotten Fleet* by John Winton, and an interview with Sir Charles Hardie, deputy chairman of Naafi, published in *Accountancy Age*. For much information on pre-Naafi canteen services to the Forces I am indebted to *Canteens in the British Army* by Sir John Fortescue, and *West and East with the EFC* by Captain E. Vredenburg. Among Naafi's archives I found E. H. Cherry's very detailed unpublished account of Naafi's part in the second world war particularly useful.

I am grateful to past and present members of Naafi who searched their memories, lent me their souvenirs and documents, and submitted so willingly to questioning. The present chairman Mr Humphrey Prideaux, the managing director Mr Edward MacGowan, the merchandise director Mr Austen Layard, and the administrative director Mr Eric Ellison, explained the structure, policy and purposes of the organisation; and former chairmen and directors Sir Lancelot Royle, Sir George Erskine, Sir William Beale and Sir Randle Feilden helped to clarify the record of their period of office. Among former Naafi executives and managers whose help I am glad to acknowledge were Messrs Frank Soden, Ernest Warner and Robert Park, and Mr Arthur Barker who read the first half of the book in manuscript and supplied helpful comments. Among present members of Naafi with whom I had interesting and instructive interviews were Messrs George Caddey, Dudley Clements, Cyril de Caux, Richard Dunn, George Hudman, Douglas Joyce, Sydney London, John Martin, Cyril Shurmer, James Tannock, Frank Walmsley, Ben White, and Miss Doris Hoare. Also, I should like to record my special appreciation of the help and advice received throughout my work from Naafi's chief public relations officer Mr Robin McKechney, and of painstaking guidance on matters of detail from Mr George Turnbull.

HARRY MILLER

PUBLISHER'S ACKNOWLEDGEMENTS

Newman Neame wish to thank the following for permission to reproduce their photographs:

ANTHONY BUCKLEY:
The colour portrait of Her Majesty The Queen

THE RADIO TIMES HULTON PICTURE LIBRARY:
Camp cooking in the Crimea, 1855
Officers' Mess of the 3rd Grenadiers, Boer War, 1899-1902
Barracks life – the officers' quarters, *circa* 1900
'Marble Arch'. Service family shopping. Suez Canal, 1951

THE IMPERIAL WAR MUSEUM:
Canadian infantry in the trenches at Ploegsteert, Flanders, 1916
The Queen's Own Cameron Highlanders in a dugout on the
   Somme, France, 1916
British troops receiving dinner rations, October 1916
Bring on the music. Naafi entertainment branch, 1942
Bring on the dancing girls. ENSA 'concert party', Egypt, 1943
British troops and a Sherman tank, Normandy, 1944
The D-Day invasion, Normandy, 1944

NORMAN L. MURRAY:
Naafi money tokens, Egypt, 1941

FOX PHOTOS LIMITED:
Troops and their 'cuppa', 1942
'Noah's Ark'. A tented canteen in the Western Desert, 1942

Finally, we should like to express our appreciation to Naafi
for its unstinted co-operation in the production of this book. We
trust it will be a source of pride to everyone and wish Naafi
bon voyage over the next fifty years of its history.

John Budden
Publishing Director
London   Newman Neame Limited

INDEX

References which do not appear as main headings may be found under the heading 'Naafi'.